Remaking
INDIA

Remaking
INDIA
One Country, One Destiny

Arun Maira

Response Books
A division of Sage Publications
New Delhi/Thousand Oaks/London

First published in 2004 by

Response Books
A division of Sage Publications India Pvt Ltd
B-42, Panchsheel Enclave
New Delhi 110 017

Sage Publications Inc	**Sage Publications Ltd**
2455 Teller Road	1 Oliver's Yard, 55 City Road
Thousand Oaks, California 91320	London EC1Y 1SP

We are grateful to R.K. Laxman for use of the eight cartoons in the book.

Published by Tejeshwar Singh for Response Books, typeset in 11/14 pts Bembo by Innovative Processors, New Delhi, and printed at Chaman Enterprises, New Delhi.

Library of Congress Cataloging-in-Publication Data

Maira, Arun.
    Remaking India: one country, one destiny/Arun Maira
        p. cm.
    Includes index.
    1. India—Economic policy—Citizen participation. 2. Sustainable develop-
ment—India—Citizen participation. 3. Industrial policy—Social aspects—
India. 4. Industrial management—Social aspects—India. 5. Values—Economic
aspects—India. 6. India—Politics and government—1977-I. Title.
HC435.2.M266   306.3'0954—dc22   2004   2004018543

We are grateful to *The Economic Times* © Bennett, Coleman & Co. Ltd., for the use of the articles in this book.

ISBN: 0–7619–3273–9 (HB)   81–7829–439–7 (India–HB)
            0–7619–3274–7 (PB)   81–7829–440–0 (India–PB)

Production Team: Roshni Basu, R.A.M. Brown and Santosh Rawat

To Shama…

Contents

Foreword *by Ratan N Tata*   9

Preface   11

1. **India Inclusive**   13
   The Real Challenge for Modern Leaders   22
   Time for a National Dialogue   25
   Business By the People, For the People   29

2. **Turning Points**   33
   An Enterprise of People   67
   In Search of Excellence in India   73

3. **Learning Fields**   77
   How to Accelerate from Zero to Sixty in
      Six Seconds   83
   The Values We Choose to Live By   86

4. **Crises of Aspiration**   91
   Looking for a Crisis of Aspiration   113
   Without Shared Visions Empires will Collapse   119

5. **Changing Our Clocks**   123
   Evolving an Idea for India   147
   Splash Around the Benefits of Growth   153

6. **New Ways**   157
    Managing India: A Single Point Plan of Action   173
    Approaches to Urban Transformation   176

7. **The Tower of Babbling**   181
    Entertainment sans Edification   196
    The 'WMD' We Really Want   199

8. **Shaping India**   207

    Bibliography   229

    Index   231

Foreword

Arun Maira has been a leader and a manager for 40 years and it has been my privilege to have been a colleague and a friend for many of those years. I first came to know him as a member of the 'learning factory' in what was then Telco, as he found his feet and then matured under that exceptional mentor—the late Sumant Moolgaokar. In his 25 years in what is now Tata Motors, Arun stood out in his ability to analyse challenges dispassionately and then inspire people to meet those challenges with a passion.

Over the last 18 years Arun has been a management consultant, first in the US and for the last four years in India as Chairman of The Boston Consulting Group. Here again, he has made his mark in his ability to analyse and articulate issues as also to provide worthwhile advice and counsel.

In *Remaking India* Arun interweaves his learnings as a practising manager and a management consultant, using the tools of organisational learning and scenario planning to make a series of propositions on how to accelerate India's development. Arun's main proposition is that the process of development in India must be inclusive—based on a vision constructed and shared by all stakeholders, evolving from a participative process of effective organisational learning and change.

The proposition he advocates is deeply insightful. As Arun argues, India has to evolve indigenously developed solutions in leveraging its three 'essential conditions'—its huge population, its diversity, and its democracy (which many see as liabilities)—to hasten its development by turning them into assets.

The book contains a set of practical suggestions for accelerating India's pace of development but essentially this is not a 'how to' book. This book is the plea of a manager to be given the chance to place his diagnosis and prescription for the country in the public domain for a genuine dialogue to take place around it. I am pleased and honoured to have the opportunity to commend whole-heartedly this slim volume from one of the country's most caring managers.

This book is a prescription from a seasoned manager on taking the country global.

Ratan N Tata

Preface

A coincidence gave birth to this book. Chapal Mehra, Managing Editor, Response Books, put the thought into my head over lunch in Kolkata that I should create a book from the articles I had been writing in *The Economic Times*, glued together with some stories from my own experiences. I was sceptical. That same afternoon, the person sitting next to me on the flight back to Mumbai also said that it was time I put together my articles and my experiences together in a book. When I landed in Mumbai, I called my wife in Delhi and told her about the coincidence. 'Don't get carried away,' she said, 'Why would anyone want to read a book with your stories and articles?' 'I don't know,' I replied, 'But how come two people in one afternoon said they would want to?' 'I hope there are others,' she said matter-of-factly. And, in truth I hope so too!

I must thank Chapal for his perseverance and thoughtful suggestions as the draft took shape. Also four others, who patiently read the first draft and helped me fine-tune the articles and experiences within the overarching theme of the book. I was very keen to get feedback from both younger and older people and so, in ascending order of age, I thank Anupam Yog of the India Brand Equity Foundation, James Abraham of The Boston Consulting Group (BCG), Satish Pradhan of Tata Sons, and N Srinivasan of the Confederation of Indian Industry (CII). They all encouraged me to overcome my hesitation about sharing my personal experiences and thus bring more heart into the book, to balance the head, which comes through in the short, intellectual articles.

For the articles, I must thank Mythili Bhusnumarth of *The Economic Times*, who invited me to write for their editorial page. The discipline of getting my thoughts on developments in India, every month, into a 1000 crisp words or less, has helped me to search for the essence in what I observe. I am grateful to *The Economic Times* © Bennett, Coleman and Co. Ltd for permission to include the articles in this book. And for the experiences that I share in this book, I have to thank those who gave me the personal challenges. Amongst these, as the book will reveal, Sumant Moolgaokar, former Chairman and architect of Tata Engineering and Locomotive Company (now Tata Motors), stands out as my greatest teacher. My family— Shama, Sunaina, and Sandeep, have played a vital role in shaping my life. My gratitude to them for their continuing love is not easy to express in words.

9 June 2004   **Arun Maira**

1
India
Inclusive

Terrific progress! In growth rate, in industry, in exports, and in exchange reserves—what a change from the miserable situation we were in!

1

India Inc*lusive*

But even where, thus, opposing interests kill,
They are to be thought of as opposing goods
Oftener than as conflicting good and ill;
Which makes the war god seem no special dunce
For always fighting on both sides at once

—Robert Frost, 'To A Young Wretch'

IN April 2004, 390 million people voted and unexpectedly changed their government, when India, the largest democracy in the world, went to the polls. The results were astounding because every analyst had predicted that the incumbent Bharatiya Janata Party (BJP) coalition government would return, and in all likelihood with an increased majority. Both national as well as the international media were full of praise for the accelerating growth of India's economy. The rising stock market was a testimony to this growth. The Congress party, then in opposition, pointed out that the shine on the country's economy, that the world was noticing was the result of reforms it had initiated more than a decade ago. However, the shine had appeared on the BJP's watch and the party claimed credit for it. Since voters usually reward the incumbent government when they are feeling good about the economy, analysts predicted the BJP would win easily.

Why did the people of India want a change in the government? One explanation was that the people wanted more inclusive development, which spread out to the rural areas and poorer sections of society, and not restricted to urban areas and the rich and middle classes who had benefited from the reforms and economic progress. Another explanation was that the people did not like the religious divisiveness fanned by the BJP and wanted to revive the secular, tolerant spirit of India. Some pointed out that regional parties were becoming more important in the electoral calculus and therefore the willingness to work with the best electoral coalitions in the states enabled the Congress to strike back at the BJP which had created a winning coalition in the previous national election. If one examines all these explanations, they point to the need for more participative governance and a more inclusive process of development. *The Times of India* (13 May 2004) said the election result was a near unanimous verdict for the politics of inclusiveness—economic, social and cultural—and against the rhetoric of divisiveness and xenophobia. According to incoming Prime Minister Manmohan Singh, people wanted 'reforms with a human face'.

But the need for inclusion brought (not unreasonable) concerns about the country's progress:

- Will the coalition government be stable?
- Will the economic reforms process be stalled by the compromises required to keep the coalition together?
- Can effective policies be framed when so many differing interests have to be reconciled?
- If the benefits of change do not come fast and reach many, the people will get dissatisfied again and throw out the incumbents. Therefore, are we not in for a long

period of frequent changes of governments that will affect the continuity and pace of reforms?

- In these circumstances, how can we get the rapid economic development we want and need for our country?

In the 1980s the Congress government under Rajiv Gandhi had begun the process of removing the shackles of bureaucracy on Indian business. It was accelerated by Finance Minister Manmohan Singh (in Narasimha Rao's cabinet) in the early 1990s. Through the 1990s, the process continued under successive coalition governments. Emerging from the shadows of control and protection, 'India Inc.' could begin to shine. Indian businesses began to modernise and compete with international companies. Consequently, Indian businessmen were given more respect by both government and society. The recent election results have made them consider what are the implications of the call for an Inclusive India on the role of India Inc. in the development of the country.

Business and nation building

The role that businesses must play in a developing society and nation has been close to my heart for about 40 years now. I had an unusual opportunity to live with this question and gather insights for most of my life: first with the Tata group in India for 25 years, then as a management consultant in the USA for 10 years, and now as Chairman, BCG, back in India for the last five years. Indian companies have a very important and difficult role to play in the country's development. It is certainly more complex than the role of corporations in developed economies. Starting much behind their international competitors, both in size and capabilities, Indian companies must rapidly learn to compete with the best in the world. At the same time, they have to compassionately connect with the conditions in their own country and the communities around them. This is by no means an easy task. The difficult question for Indian businesses is how to pursue improvement in business performance and effectively enrich the lives of people around them, not as separate activities but in a mutually reinforcing process that improves results on both sides. Perhaps some of the guiding ideas Indian companies need for their management could be different from the ideas that work for successful companies centred in economically advanced countries, because their social and economic environments are entirely different.

My consulting work in the USA brought me in touch with some leading intellectuals and practitioners in the field of organisational learning. My objective as a consultant is to enable people to work together to produce the results they want. Therefore, whatever the subject of my consulting engagement— whether it is the development of a new strategy, or change in mindsets in the organisation—I find the concepts and principles of organisational learning invaluable. A strategy, to be effective, has to be understood by and committed to by its key stakeholders and the people it affects and must guide their actions and behaviours. Mindsets can be changed by facilitating change in the ideas and principles guiding behaviours of people in the organisation. In both cases, prevalent ideas have to be unlearned and new ideas learned and applied in the organisation—which is basically the process of organisational learning.

When I observe developments in India through the lens of organisational learning, I can see that the country is searching for new approaches to govern change that will fit the changed conditions in India. Incidentally, Indian business corporations are also working for the same kind of change. However, the method and momentum of previous approaches continues. Politically, India has moved from an era of a one-party dominated government to coalition governments. State politics and governments have become more independent of the centre.

Also, sections of Indian society, which could previously be excluded from the process of decision-making, such as the so-called 'backward classes', have to be included, not merely as beneficiaries of development but as participants with power to determine the direction of change. The second phase of economic reforms requires changes in policies that directly affect the masses—such as subsidies, labour laws, prices of utilities, and taxation of farmers' incomes. This makes decision-making at a policy level more complex than in the first phase of reforms that mostly affected industry. These changes require new approaches for leadership and management.

I have been reflecting on the need for new approaches for leadership and change in India in articles that I have written in *The Economic Times* and Indian business journals over the years. It is clear that processes of decision-making, planning, and implementing change that may have been effective earlier in India cannot be effective any longer. New ways must be used that are appropriate to the changed conditions. For example, a directive, centralised planning process, with experts determining the targets and allocation of resources cannot be an effective model. Now more participative processes are required for dialogue and decision-making by which diverse interests can be understood and aligned to the larger whole. Besides, when governments and leaders change frequently, top-down visions cannot have continuity and so lose their power rapidly. Therefore, visions have to be developed by a broad consensus involving many people to enable continuity of the change process. However, the underlying philosophy and procedures of management do not appear to have changed enough to fit the new conditions of India, and new processes required are yet to be instituted.

In this book I propose a way, founded on principles of organisational learning, for India to accelerate change and development that fits the Indian conditions in which the change has to be brought about. Let me be clear at the outset: this book does not present a vision for India in terms of the size of the country's economy and its various sectors. Nor does it recommend economic strategies for bringing about growth. Therefore, readers looking for an economic vision or prescription will be disappointed. But the book does very strongly advocate a solution for India. The solution is a process for inclusive development founded on the development of a shared vision. The thesis of this book is that the vision of the outcome of change that people desire must be created through participation. Further, an agreement on the way this will be brought about must be the result of a participative process of effective organisational learning and change. Therefore, to guess, or even worse, to prescribe, the vision that should be the outcome of this process would be antithetical to the core proposition of this book.

The book recommends a framework of concepts and techniques for a participative process of change. It intersperses short conceptual pieces with stories from my own experiences to illustrate the relevance of these concepts. These concepts are derived from a selection of articles I have written in *The Economic Times* as I observed developments in the country. And since short articles cannot fully explain the meaning of abstract concepts, I have substantially expanded on the basic themes of some of these articles, thus giving them life and meaning through stories of how they have applied in my experience.

The book is an unfolding story of learning. The first two chapters explain my views on India's current situation and 'where I am coming from' by recounting some critical moments in my own learning journey. Chapter three describes the Learning Field, which is the organising framework for the ideas in the book. The next four chapters explain, through articles and stories, the relevance and meaning of concepts in each of the four domains in the Learning Field. The eighth and last chapter is neither an epilogue nor the end of the story. It is an invitation to readers to participate and continue the story of change in India by applying the ideas from the earlier chapters. I hope that readers will find these ideas useful to make change happen, whatever be their spheres of responsibility.

A picture can sometimes say more than a 1000 words. This book is about change (or the lack of it), leadership (or the lack of it), and the inclusion of the common man in the process of development. These are themes that RK Laxman, India's most eminent cartoonist, has commented on brilliantly over the past 50 years. Therefore, with his permission, I have used his cartoons to start each chapter.

The structure of the book is like a necklace with the stories providing the thread on which all the conceptual beads are strung and connected. Each concept, like the beads, has value by itself, and similarly the articles, describing the concepts applied to India, can be read independently if the reader wishes. And the stories, like the thread, have an integrity of their own and some reappear after intervening articles to continue through in following chapters. They could also be read on their own, ignoring the articles if the reader wishes. However, as in a necklace, the combination of the thread and beads—the stories and articles—creates something better, I hope. The pendant is the last chapter, Shaping India, where all the concepts come together, like colours from all the beads.

The Real Challenge for
Modern Leaders

*A new model of a leader is required to build and lead
coalitions of people with diverse beliefs and needs*

SEPTEMBER 2001 was a month of bad news. An Indian national
daily carried a front-page report of a starving Oriya family who
sold two children to a journalist for Rs 1100 and 15 kg of rice.
It was their only hope to save the children and the rest of the
family from starving to death. The same week the head of
ICICI reported that the perennial stream of requests for project
financing had dried up. The economy had stalled, he said. The
banks had funds but there were no takers. Speaking on the
same platform a well known economist sounded alarmed that
there was insufficient liquidity in the secondary capital market
causing share prices to fall. He urged that money be released
into the stock markets. Same country; same economy; three
vignettes. The question is: 'Which is the real economy and
what is the problem we are trying to solve?'

Article first published in *The Economic Times.*

A few days earlier, an international management consultancy had presented a 13-point plan for the Indian economy to the Prime Minister. It pointed mostly to the same areas of action that the Finance Minister had outlined in his budget proposals in February, the only significant difference being on the need for labour reforms. *Yeh sab kaise hoga?* was the Prime Minister's question to the consultancy. His point was that we do not need another reminder of what needs to be done. We have known it for some time. The question is 'how'.

Shortly after the terrorist attacks of September 11, Donald Rumsfeld, the US Secretary of Defense said in an interview that the USA would smoke out the perpetrators of the carnage in New York wherever they were hiding. Replying to the question as to whether there had been a security failure, he said that it was impossible to avoid such an action 'in an open society in which anyone, anywhere, using any technique can cause terror'. The next few days were very sobering for the leaders of the free world. *The Economist* advised them in an article titled 'Allies in Search of a Strategy' to 'first build the coalition, then think what to do'.

There is a common thread in these stories of poverty in India and terror in the world. It is this: Leaders of open societies in which there is great diversity of perceptions and needs have to be very skilful in building coalitions. The broader the diversity of stakeholders in the issue, the greater the need for skills in aligning their actions. Therefore, the key to the solution of seemingly intractable problems such as terrorism, poverty, and environmental degradation may lie in the 'process of engaging stakeholders', rather than the battle plans of experts.

The ideals of an open society, built on the rights of individuals and democracy, claimed a major victory at the end of the last millennium. The collapse of the closed societies behind the iron curtain left the stage to Western democracies, with the

USA as their proud leader. Within the developing world, India has been struggling to live by the ideals of freedom and democracy for more than half a century now. The war for an ideology may have been won, but we need the practical means to live by this ideology while fulfilling more basic human needs. Paramount amongst these is the need for physical security, which requires a 'war' on terrorism. Another is the need for food, which requires a 'war' on poverty.

To win these wars we may have to discard ideas of leadership that have served society well for hundreds of years. These modern wars cannot be won by commanders-in-chief who require that their orders are followed without question, and therefore require a state of emergency so they can be granted the right to suppress dissent. But it will not be easy to acknowledge that we need a new model of leadership. The hero as a model of leadership has served society well for centuries, albeit in different circumstances. When danger threatens, as it does now, it is our instinct to pick up whatever weapons we have at hand, even if they are not appropriate. What we really need though are leaders who can work without strong authority, blend the interests of many diverse people and yet deliver results fast. A democratic framework requires such leadership. There is a chicken-and-egg situation here. If we do not have effective democratic institutions, we have to take recourse to dictatorial leaders. But dictatorial leaders further weaken democratic institutions by which they feel shackled. So where does the answer lie?

Therefore the answer to the question, *Yeh sab kaise hoga?* lies in effective participatory processes. And the task before twenty-first century leaders, whether in India or the USA, is to understand and adopt this new kind of leadership. Such leadership can build strong institutions and processes that open societies need to win so-called 'wars' that require participation of people with widely different beliefs.

Time for a National Dialogue

It is necessary to establish a process for dialogue amongst contending parties and develop agreement on a few essential principles they will adhere to in the nation's interests

W E have a new government. Will this be the spring of our hope or the winter of our discontent? Till recently we were obsessed with looking East at China and lamenting that India had missed the boat. Then came our President, APJ Abdul Kalam, who travelled the country and told our children about India's recent achievements. Not the greatness of the India that was centuries ago, but the seeds of greatness in the India that is. His story was one of hope. Arun Shourie, veteran journalist and parlimentarian, wrote about some of our impressive achievements in industry and science, something which Dr Mashelkar, one of India's pioneering scientists, also spoke about at the Delhi University convocation. Some cynics say that the achievements these leaders extol, though impressive, are few and limited mostly to science and industry. Look at the poverty and filth and disorganisation and corruption, they say.

Article first published in *The Economic Times*.

When will India ever be rid of it? Speaking to the Society of Indian Automobile Manufacturers, who were glowing in the upswing of sales in the first half of this year, Finance Secretary, Mr Naryanan drew attention to our sudden mood swings. Our cricketers are revered like gods the day after they win and reviled like villains the next week when they lose. We go from despair to euphoria, winter to spring, and back again very easily.

I feel strongly that our country is at a turning point. The choice now is either to build on the rising hope and accelerate change, or allow ourselves to slip back into frustrated helplessness. Undoubtedly, there is a great deal to be done. India's size and diversity makes our task larger and more complex than anywhere else in the world. But the size of the task should not intimidate us, but spur us to look for innovative solutions. The sheer size of our population, of a billion people and more, with millions of poor and illiterate, is a problem that staggers economists. How much resources will we need to improve the situation for these people and where will these resources come from? The diversity of our people, their differing economic status, religions, languages, and political affiliations, bedevils efforts to obtain alignment. How can such diverse peoples be united towards a common cause? But, as often, the seeds of the solution are in the problem itself.

The first step is that we have to stop thinking of our people as liabilities and convert them into our assets. For example, India can be the largest knowledge and skill-based service provider to the world within the next two decades, just as China seems to have become the largest provider of low-cost manufactures. Thereby we can bring in around $200 billion additional revenues to India every year and generate an additional 40 million jobs. However, I will not dwell on this example of how our large population can be our competitive advantage. What we need to do before that is to focus on the *process* of engaging masses of people to accelerate the changes they want in this country. In this process of engagement, I believe, lies the key to our seemingly intractable problems.

Three changes are essential to convert people from being the problem to becoming part of the solution. The first is to create a contagion of hope. Leaders proposing a vision for the country and propagating stories of success are sparking hope, which is essential to start a transformation of attitudes. The second is to engage people with helping themselves, thereby overcoming the helplessness that pervades us in the face of problems we feel are beyond our control. With this approach, villages in Rajasthan have found solutions to chronic water deficiency and communities in Bangalore are taking charge of improvements to their localities in cooperation with the municipal authorities. Similarly, several schemes of involving communities in innovative ways of providing education at minimal cost are demolishing economic equations of how much money is required to provide education to India's children.

However, even these two changes together will not ensure the transformation we want. The third and the most essential change is to create alignment amongst many perspectives. We are blessed—or cursed, some would say—with diversity. This richness can be a blessing if we can work together effectively. But if we cannot, which too often seems to be the case, we may not realise our vision. Political parties espouse one thing when in power and the opposite when they are not, merely to trip the government of the day. We must have alignment on a few fundamental goals and principles. These will form the bridge to take us across to the land on the other side—a land without poverty that stands tall and mightily respected amongst nations. In a democracy there will always be disagreement and debate. Therefore, we will jostle on the bridge as we move across it. But while trying to beat others and get ahead of them, let us not unwittingly damage the bridge itself. For then, we will all fall down.

We need a productive dialogue amongst leaders representing diverse stakeholders in our society. This dialogue will have two purposes. The first is to develop a shared vision of the nation that we are aiming to become. The second is to agree on the few fundamental strategies that we will have to follow. To many this may seem simplistic and I agree it will not be easy to get the meeting of hearts and minds that is needed. Participants will be cynical, suspicious of each other's motives, and unable to really listen to others. If we want to make this dialogue successful, let us take advantage of lessons learned in our country and elsewhere in conducting such mission critical dialogues. For example, in South Africa, when the country seemed to be on the brink of collapse, blacks and whites, capitalists and communists, sat together and worked out a vision for a new nation. They also worked out the principles of the transition process. What makes me more hopeful for our country now is that some people are actively exploring how to induce such a productive dialogue in India, cutting across differences in income levels, occupations, and political affiliations. This process of dialogue is the third leg of the stool, on which, with vision and empowerment, we can raise a great democratic nation.

Business By the People,
For the People

The role of business corporations in society cannot be limited to producing wealth for their shareholders, which was a dangerously narrow-minded view that became ascendant in the 1990s in the USA and spread elsewhere

T HE struggle between private capitalism and state socialism through the twentieth century seemed over in 1989 with the collapse of the erstwhile Soviet Union. The verdict was that business should be conducted by the people and not the state. The celebration of the victory of the capitalist ideology was, however soon marred by the corporate scandals in the USA. People became concerned that the capitalist establishment was focussed on its own privileges and not the interests of the common man. With due apologies to Fukuyama, the history of ideology had not ended. In a recent book, *20:21 Vision: Twentieth Century Lessons for the Twenty-First Century,* Bill Emmott, Editor-in-Chief of *The Economist,* asks capitalists to ponder why, if

Article first published in *The Economic Times.*

capitalism is so obviously the best solution, it has been challenged more than once. He wonders if communism is the last challenge or there will be another. The true battle, he says, is within capitalism itself.

The principal tool of private capitalism is the limited liability company. Companies are created to serve the needs of their shareholders; and, according to some, only the needs of their shareholders. In this narrow but ascendant ideology of the 1990s, the business corporation's only business was business with no obligation to provide other services to the community. This view is being increasingly questioned and until there is agreement on what is the proper role of the company in society, there cannot be agreement on the right measurements of the performance of companies and their leaders. In fact, the debate about corporate governance following the scandals in the USA ignores this overarching issue altogether. The focus of that debate has been the relationship between managers and shareholders of companies and the role of boards in protecting the interests of shareholders.

The more important issue is the relationship between companies and society. In their excellent book, *The Company: A Short History of a Revolutionary Idea*, Micklethwait and Wooldridge, who work with *The Economist*, trace the birth and evolution of the concept of the limited liability company. They point out that, 'No matter how much modern businessmen may presume to the contrary, the company was a political creation (which) existed because it had been given a license to do so, and granted the privilege of limited liability.' Society, through its political organs, granted this unprecedented privilege to protect the interests of investors. But, to retain their license to operate, companies must look beyond investors' interests and be responsive to society's broader needs.

Some businessmen in India and elsewhere have understood these needs and are doing this. Their work in this regard is sometimes called corporate social responsibility, which has been breezily described by *The Economist*, in a recent issue, as the greatest fad of the 1990s! Even though other writers with the same paper, as already mentioned here, suggest that it is time to ponder on the role of business in society. For Indian businessmen, this is a vital question. Indian businesses have recently acquired more freedom and respect from society, and are more vulnerable to domestic socio-political reactions than their counterparts in the West. There is greater need in India, than in the West, to build systems to serve the societal needs for health care, education, and the like. However, current news and views in Indian business journals and largely in the media would suggest to the common man that the business sector is withdrawing from filling the gap. He hears that private sector companies are curtailing their welfare programmes to concentrate on their core business activities. And that public sector companies, whose charter required them to promote employment generation and welfare of the communities in which they operated, are becoming an endangered species. Perhaps it is time for Indian business to declare its agenda for fulfilling society's expectations and be seen to live up to it.

The three areas for companies' engagement with society are:

- *The physical environment:* Preserving and/or improving it—avoiding pollution, increasing forestation, etc.
- *The social environment:* Engaging with communities' needs for services such as education, health, water, infrastructure.
- *The political environment:* Influencing the process of improvement in public policy and governance.

The agreement about business's proper role, and clarity about legitimate ways to fulfil it, diminishes as we move down from the first to the third area. By now it is widely accepted almost everywhere that business should not be left unchecked to spoil the physical environment. The subjects of ongoing discussion between governments, businesses and NGOs are appropriate standards and rules, useful technologies, and means for reducing costs and making profits while protecting or enhancing the environment.

Business's proper role in the social agenda is less clear—though the need for business to contribute is increasingly accepted. One theme that runs through this agenda is philanthropy. This essentially suggests that engagement with social development is a matter of choice, depending on personal values of owners and managers as well as the amount of surplus generated by their business, whereas protecting the environment is no longer philanthropy—it is a business necessity with penalties for failure whether or not the business makes a profit. However, even businesses that are committed to social causes must find the best ways to have maximum impact. Should they create independent trusts, donate money to causes, or manage their own programmes?

The most contentious issue is whether business can have or should have any role in influencing the political environment. Business is often blamed by society if it does nothing, as Shell was, when the Nigerian government executed Ken Saro-Wiwa. On the other hand, if they do speak out, business leaders can be accused of meddling, as they were in India after the Gujarat riots. The question is not only whether business should or should not have a role, but also how it should play that role effectively. Since the contract between business and society is not clear, misunderstandings will continue until the contract is clarified.

However, failure to reach a consensus on its role (in any of the three areas) can cost business dearly, through breakdown in trust and damage to reputations, in addition to financial costs, if and when a calamity takes place and society feels an unwritten contract was breached. Therefore, it behoves business leaders to proactively engage civil society and government in a constructive dialogue to confirm what society should fairly expect from them. If they wish to be seen as leaders of desirable change in society, businessmen should take the lead to establish this dialogue.

2

Turning

Points

You are not included in the cabinet? Good! Now you can devote your time to the welfare of the nation which you wanted to do always!

2

Turning Points

I shall be telling this with a sigh
Somewhere ages and ages hence:
Two roads diverged in a wood, and I—
I took the one less travelled by,
And that has made all the difference

—Robert Frost, 'The Road Not Taken'

A writer's point of view is influenced by his beliefs. His beliefs in turn are shaped by the experiences in his life. As I look back on my life, I can see three significant turning points at which I chose to follow unconventional paths. The choices I made may illuminate my beliefs, and my point of view, both as a professional and as a person. It is through this perspective that I observe the change in India.

I returned to India from the USA in January 2000. My wife and I had left behind two children, a beautiful house in a lovely town, her creative ceramics practice, and my rewarding work as a management consultant in a booming US economy. Friends in India seemed surprised that we came back at all. In comparison with what you had in the USA, what is it about India that brings you back? they asked.

I was not surprised to hear what they said. Their reactions had been the same when I had suddenly decided to leave a very successful career in one of India's most admired companies—Telco (now Tata Motors)—in 1989 to go to the USA, exchanging a high position and the security of a company I had worked with for 25 years for a new job in a new profession in a new organisation and in a new country. Both these decisions seemed to cause people endless wonder.

However, to understand what motivated me to choose the path less travelled at these forks in the road, I must go back to the first fork, way back in 1964.

The India that I knew

In 1964, I graduated with a master's degree in physics from St Stephen's College in Delhi. I was not yet 21 and my whole life was an adventure yet to unfold. Bright-eyed and brimming with the enthusiasm of youth, I was ready to play my part to change the world. India as a nation was even younger. It was only 17 years since the birth of independent India. The young country was enthusiastically looking forward to its 'tryst with destiny', in Jawaharlal Nehru's memorable words. There was hope and idealism in the air at campuses such as St Stephen's, and the best and brightest were ready to serve their country. Prior to India's independence, goals for the country's development, whatever they were, had been set by the British. A popular view that fuelled the movement for independence was that Britain had used India for its own ends: The British had used India as a source of raw materials for its own industries and discouraged development of Indian industry. With independence, Indians could choose their own goals for the country's development. Mahatma Gandhi had wanted India to develop its villages where the vast majority of its people lived.

Jawaharlal Nehru, the first Prime Minister of independent India, however, had a different plan. He wanted India to be modern and industrial, and thus a country that would count amongst the nations of the world. He adopted the Soviet model of central planning to direct resources towards national objectives. This required a cadre of professional administrators to govern the country and also to represent its interests abroad. The British Indian Civil Service (ICS) provided a model that the country was familiar with. Members of the service, which the British had opened up to Indians also, were highly respected. Most Indians who joined the ICS had been to Cambridge or Oxford, an education that very few Indians could afford. However, selection was based on merit which was evaluated through a rigorous process. Therefore, the members of the ICS were considered the elite of the country because while they had a privileged social background, they had also been rigorously tested for their qualities of leadership. But these were a small group and the nation's new agenda of development required many more of its bright young people to be recruited into the public services. Thus, the Indian Administrative Service (IAS) and the Indian Foreign Service (IFS) were created to provide the administrators and diplomats the country needed. These services were open to all Indians. Merit was the only criteria and it was as strictly assessed as it had been for the ICS.

A plan for the future

By the mid-1960s, a framework for independent India's development had emerged. Indian industrialists had recommended, in their own so-called 'Bombay Plan' for the development of the country, a mixed economy with both the private sector and government playing parts. Their plan required government to play a central role in creating public sector enterprises in capital-intensive sectors. There was a consensus that while the private sector could grow, the government should build the commanding heights of the Indian economy. Dams, power stations, even nuclear reactors were built. Indian Institutes of Technology (IITs), steel plants, and other industries were set up in different parts of the country with assistance from the USA, UK, Germany, and the Soviet Union. In the 1960s, the country was busy building and modernising. The disappointment with the performance of the public sector and cynicism about the role of government in the development of the economy came only much later, not only in India, but even Britain which had also taken a similar course of heavy government involvement in large industry, and, even later, in the Soviet Union where the private sector had been totally eliminated.

In the 1960s, the elite government services, the IAS and IFS, attracted the best and brightest in the country. These services provided young Indians a career of immense prestige and an avenue to serve the nation. Young men selected into these services were considered to be the most eligible bachelors in the country! No wonder, almost the entire graduating class of St Stephen's in 1964 and the years before and after, in history, economics and even the sciences, joined the IAS and IFS. That was where I was headed as well. However, there was a small problem: I was underage to sit for the examination along with the rest of my class and had to wait another year.

Since I was at a loose end, the principal of St Stephen's suggested I go to interviews with business organisations in Calcutta and Bombay (as the cities were called then). I turned up my nose. In those days, business was not considered a respectable vocation and my peers in St Stephen's would have been horrified if I, with my good record, were to stoop down to join a business organisation. Business was not held in high esteem in India then. It was not just socialist rhetoric that was hurting the image of business then as much as the behaviour of the business community itself. As early as 1957, 10 years after the country's independence, a former president of the Federation of Indian Chambers of Commerce and Industry (FICCI) had admitted:

We have failed to win the confidence of the people and identify ourselves with the awakening of the masses to the consciousness of poverty and degradation and the insistent demand for a better life. The general impression we have made on the masses is that we are intoxicated with power and wealth, indulge in its vulgar show, and that our sole aim in life is to amass fortunes for ourselves regardless of national interests.

This state of affairs led to several inquiry commissions in the next few years into the state of affairs in the private corporate sector: the Vivian Bose Commission, the Monopolies Inquiry Commission, the Dutt Industrial Policy Enquiry Committee and the Wanchoo Committee. Their reports led to the further fall of the business community in public esteem.

The principal of St Stephen's managed to persuade me that I had nothing to lose by going to these interviews. I had not visited Calcutta and Bombay until then and the offer was tempting. I would travel first class and stay in fine hotels. Besides, I was under no obligation to accept a job. Why not? I thought. My interview in Calcutta was easy. I was received by the company's CEO who looked at my record and the principal's letter and offered me a job on the spot. The salary and perquisites he described were astonishing for a poor college student who had been calibrating his expectations around Rs 400 a month starting salary of the IAS and IFS. Big salary, an apartment, a car, club membership, holidays! 'The salary is mostly pocket money', the CEO suggested. And what a fortune that pocket money was!

I asked what work I would do. The CEO took me into the tea-tasting room near his office and showed me that I would, like the other men in white coats in the room, swivel tea in my mouth and spit it out. Fortunately this work was only half-day, the afternoons being free for golf and recreation. What a great deal, some might think—a huge compensation for little work. But my negative impressions about a career in business were reinforced. This job was not for me, with my idealist notions of 'serving the country'.

My next interview, in Bombay, was with the Tata Administrative Services (TAS). The Tatas were already beginning to stand apart from other business organisations in the public mind. They had left FICCI in protest when its president, who was one of the businessmen indicted for malpractice by an inquiry commission, did not step aside. The selection process for the TAS was rigorous. A panel of Tata directors spent three full days with the candidates. They explored what each of us did well and what we aspired to do. Professor Choksi, Chairman of the panel, said the directors knew that I was biding time to sit for the public service examination. They respected my calling to contribute to the country. They explained the history of the Tata Group and the philosophy of its founder, Jamsetji Tata. I was quite impressed and realised that there were many ways to serve the country. Though Tatas was a business organisation, it was helping very tangibly to build India. And so, in 1964, I took a decision to take the road less travelled and unlike my peers, joined a business organisation, the House of Tatas, rather than the public services.

The Tatas

I realised the great respect people in India had for the Tatas when I returned from a business trip to Singapore in 1969. At that time, travel abroad was a rare privilege for an Indian. I had a daily allowance of nine pounds, which is all the Indian government would allow, to pay for my hotel, meals and transportation. However, thanks to the 'all you can eat for two Singapore dollars' deal at the Komala Villas restaurant and using public transport as much as possible, I could save a little money with which to buy a large number of gee-gaws, at a few cents each from the Chinese Government Emporium in Singapore, to bring back for the staff in the office.

I landed at Santa Cruz airport with my large bag of gifts and a list to show that their total cost was just under the Rs 500 customs allowance. The customs agent at the airport would not accept my word. Much to my embarrassment the contents of my bag were spilled onto the table and all the little gee-gaws were examined before an increasingly impatient queue of people behind me. The hold-up brought a customs officer to the scene. He inquired as to what the matter was. His colleague apprised him of the situation with a 'let's get him' look. The officer asked me where I worked. I said with the Tatas. The response stunned me. 'If this gentleman says he has spent less than Rs 500, he has spent less than Rs 500,' said the officer to the agent. 'He works for the Tatas, and Tata people always tell the truth'. That was the reputation of the Tatas even then when business people in India were generally suspected of cheating in quality and price to make a gain for themselves.

I spent a very fulfilling 25 years with the Tatas. It was the best business school I could have attended at the time. The Tata's goal was to grow businesses and make profits and also contribute to nation building. I was challenged to think broadly and work efficiently to produce profits while building communities and environments. Most of my years were with Telco—the truck manufacturing and engineering company in the Tata group. And most of those years were at Telco's new factory in Pune where the company established its engineering development centre and machine and tool building facilities, which enabled Telco to later expand into light trucks and cars. The scale of expansion was huge and in the words of Sumant Moolgaokar, CEO of Telco, 'we were not only building trucks in Pune but an entire industry.'

Telco's Pune factory was both a celebration and an indictment of India's approach to industrial development. Through the 1950s and 1960s, Indians were learning new technologies and new skills to catch up with the industrialised countries. Telco was one of the finest examples of the newfound confidence amongst Indians. Telco had learned to build trucks and buses from Mercedes Benz. By the time Telco's 15-year technical collaboration agreement with Mercedes ended in 1969, the company was turning out vehicles to Mercedes' international standards with almost 100 per cent Indian content. By then, all the German engineers and managers had left, replaced by Indians. The only German who remained behind was the chief of quality. Mercedes seemed fully satisfied with the quality of the vehicles made by the Indian team at Jamshedpur and exported them to nearby countries such as Malaysia and Sri Lanka, confidently wearing the famous Mercedes Benz star on their grill.

By the early 1970s, as Telco was advancing, problems with India's industrial development strategy began to show up. The country was running out of foreign exchange. As a result of this, imports of many vital inputs for industry were banned, and the government hoped to provide these from Indian public sector companies. For instance, the special machine tools Telco required for its Pune factory could only come from government's Hindustan Machine Tools, which was then just learning how to produce such machines that had been imported until then. This would be a bottleneck in completing Telco's plans in Pune. Indeed, several such bottlenecks plagued Indian industry. Telco, however, could not take the risk of faulty machinery and so it decided to design and manufacture its own machine tools. Similarly, when

Telco was not permitted to import equipment for its new foundry, it had to learn how to make foundry equipment on its own. No other truck manufacturer in the world made its own machine tools and foundry equipment. But Telco had to, if it wanted to proceed with its plans. Thus Telco added costs, but also learned new engineering and manufacturing skills, the benefit of which showed up later when the company began to diversify its range of commercial vehicles into lighter segments and finally, cars.

Telco's Pune factory must be one of the rare examples in the world of the growth of an ecology along with the growth of a factory, rather than the despoiling of ecology that factories are notorious for. In my office was a picture of the land that the Tatas were given to build the factory. It was barren, stony, and without even a bush as far as the eye could see. The land had been a forest a 100 years back that was denuded by cattle and people. Year after year as I looked out of my office window in Pune, I would see more factory buildings on what had been that barren land, along with more and more trees and birds. The ecology developed so well that in 1986 a panther delivered a litter in a dense grove of trees within the factory walls!

VS Naipaul, the Nobel Prize winning author, was struck by the emerging confidence of young Indians in Telco's new factory in Pune. Naipaul had taken a very despondent view of India in his book, *India: An Area of Darkness.* In a later book, *India: A Wounded Civilization,* published in 1977, he saw no reason to change this view. However, one passage in this book stands out, different in tone and hope to the rest, when Naipaul describes his visit to Telco's factory in Pune the previous year. He writes:

The plateau around Pune is now in parts like a new country, a new continent. It provides uncluttered space, and space is what the factory-builders and the machine-makers say they need; they say they are building for the twenty-first century. Their confidence, in the general doubt, is staggering. But it is so in India: the doers are always enthusiastic. And industrial India is a world away from the India of bureaucrats and journalists and theoreticians. The men who make and use machines— and the Indian industrial revolution is increasingly Indian: more and more of the machines are made in India— glory in their new skills. Industry in India is not what industry is said to be in other parts of the world. It has its horrors, but in spite of Gandhi, it does not—in the context of India—dehumanize. An industrial job in India is more than just a job. Men handling new machines, technical skills that to them are new, can also discover themselves as men, as individuals.

The Indian economy was constricted further through the 1970s by the policies and rules of politicians and bureaucrats. The binding began in Nehru's era of planned development. However, it began to suffocate in the 1970s when Indira Gandhi ruled. A popular view is that the Indian economy was 'unbound', in writer Gurcharan Das's words, in 1991 with the emergency liberalisation measures taken by the then Finance Minister, Dr Manmohan Singh, when the country's foreign exchange resources had run so low that India came within hours of a default on its loan repayments. However, few know that the process of opening up the economy to foreign investments and new competition had begun earlier, in the 1980s, in some sectors such as automobiles. Hence Telco was amongst the first Indian companies to stand up to foreign competition in the 1980s while, at the same time, struggling with the shackles of control by Indian bureaucrats on the economy that had, by then, become onerous and even absurd.

Prime Minister Rajiv Gandhi began opening up the Indian economy to the world in the 1980s. Several Japanese companies were permitted to manufacture and sell light commercial vehicles in India. With their entry, Telco's ambitions to grow faced a powerful threat. Telco wanted to compete with them but its hands were tied. Telco's licence permitted it to produce commercial vehicles above 6 tonnes gross weight only. The Japanese were entering the market with lighter vehicles, a segment where the market was expected to grow more rapidly. The irony was that Telco had now to plead with the bureaucracy to permit it to compete with foreign manufacturers in India! Who was the Indian bureaucracy protecting from whom? The Japanese from Telco? Finally, after much debate with the bureaucrats, Telco was given permission to design and produce a vehicle below 6 tonnes. Harnessing all its newly learned abilities to design vehicles, machine tools and dies, Telco took on and beat back the Japanese.

Leaving home

While the Pune factory was growing, I was learning and growing too and so was my family. Our two children started and finished their school years in Pune. I saw very little of them though. This was because the state of Maharashtra, along with many other parts of the country, was beginning to be plagued by chronic power shortages, which was another failure of India's planned development. Maharashtra staggered the days on which factories would work to mitigate the shortages. Telco's factory worked on Saturdays and Sundays, when our children were home from school, and was closed on Thursdays when they were at school. Besides there was much to be done and working hours were long. My daughter called me an 'absentee father'. Upon finishing school, she went on a scholarship to college in the USA. A year later she got very ill and though she stabilised, she required good care. My wife was anxious to be with her in the USA. Meanwhile my son had also finished school and wanted to go to college in the USA.

I was torn between my commitment to my work on one hand, and on the other my concern for my daughter and the strong desire to be with my children who I had not known enough and who were going further away. I shared my dilemma with my mentor, Sumant Moolgaokar, the Chairman of Telco. All who were privileged to be close to him knew him as a very kind and wise man besides being one of India's greatest industrial leaders. Moolgaokar told me that for the sake of Telco, he could not let me go. But he understood my dilemma and also asked me to consider my obligations to my family. With these thoughts, he turned me over to our Chairman, JRD Tata. JRD pointed out to me that whereas Telco may find other managers to fill the void, my daughter and son had only one father. And the void I may leave in their lives could not be filled by anyone else. JRD also made my decision easier by offering me a sabbatical and suggesting that if I worked with an international consulting company in the USA, I may be more useful to the Tatas and India on my return. Ratan Tata had just then taken over in Telco from Moolgaokar. He had been a warm friend to me and my wife when he and I were colleagues in Tata Steel at the start of my career with the Tatas. He was sorry that I had to leave, but felt that some years abroad would give me an international perspective that he was keen to bring into the Tata Group. That's how, with guidance from three wise leaders, I plunged into the road towards the less familiar, to work in the USA.

In the USA, I found myself in a new country, a new organisation, and even a new profession. The transition was neither simple nor painless. I had to now learn social and business conventions that were often unfamiliar to me as I consulted with clients in the US, South America, and Europe. I struggled with the challenge to my ability, to influence change in organisations in which I did not have the authority I had acquired in Tatas over 25 years. Therefore, I found my personal learning agenda—my search for concepts and skills—increasingly focussed on how organisations change; how leaders enable organisations to change; and how an external facilitator can accelerate the change that an organisation and its leaders may desire or need.

The questions uppermost in my mind, as I began my new career in consulting in the USA, were: Why would an American company want to take the advice of a middle-aged executive whose only qualification in management was 25 years of experience with an Indian company? This, especially in 1989, when Indian industry, if known at all in the USA, had a reputation only for poor quality and inefficiency. And how could I add value to my clients in the USA with my experience in Tatas?

My first consulting assignment was with an American automobile parts' manufacturing company. Japanese automobile manufacturers had shaken up American industry in the 1980s. Americans were worried about the 'hollowing out' of American manufacturing and disappearance of jobs. Many US companies were struggling. The American company that had hired Arthur D Little Inc., the consultancy I joined in the USA, had recently been bought over by a German engineering company. The new German CEO's first priority was to downsize the US operations. His targets were two old plants, one in Detroit, the other in Philadelphia. His worries were the contingent liabilities for environmental cleanups and the public relations backlash against a German company throwing Americans out of work, especially in inner city Detroit and Philadelphia. He wanted a reputed American consulting company to endorse his decision and prepare a plan to manage the risks in closing down the two plants.

My colleagues and I began with a deeper question: What would it take to make the two plants competitive? And to answer this, we wanted to understand why the plants were not able to compete. While my younger colleagues, those with the MBAs, pored over the company's reports and financial statements, I went out to 'rub my nose on the shop floor'. Sumant Moolgaokar had taught me, when he sent me out at a very young age to manage Tatas' factories in Pune that to understand what was really going on in a factory, I should first get to 'the real place, see real things, and talk to real people'. So I showed up in the late night shifts in Detroit and Philadelphia, talked to older black workers and union representatives, many of whom had been with the company for decades and were now fearful of losing their jobs. To them, I was a curiosity—a stranger from a country they hardly knew. While they did not identify easily with me, I also seemed to be very different from their bosses. They sensed I knew a lot about running a factory but, unlike their bosses, I said little and mostly listened to them. To their concerns, fears and hopes. Their analysis of the situation. Their complaints about management's unwillingness to make investments to improve the factory. And their suggestions for change.

In the day shifts I went to the executives in their offices and listened to their complaints about how the union was destroying the company and the difficulty in getting cooperation from the workmen. They said they were working as hard as they could to improve quality and productivity. But they acknowledged that the rate of improvement was not sufficient to save the plants. The boat was sinking faster than they could bail water. As I listened and learned through those days and nights, I pieced together a picture of officers and sailors on a ship wrestling with each other while their ship was sinking.

My colleagues and I presented the CEO with the plan he had asked for. We acknowledged that the company was on a sinking trajectory. We quantified the improvement in the company's financial position that could be obtained if the plants were closed. But we also estimated the huge risks to the company's customer relations and public image.

We also surprised the CEO with an alternative plan. The seeds of this plan came from my conversations with the workmen and managers. The plan had benefits for all parties. Most workmen, though not all, could retain their jobs, as could most managers. The union's victory would be the change in the management's decision to close the plants. And the CEO would get the improvement required in financial performance without the risks to the German company's public image in the USA if it closed the plants. This alternative plan was built upon a series of changes to be made by the management, unions, and workmen, and the improvements in quality, productivity, and financial performance of the company that would only be achieved if they worked together.

The key to the breakthrough was a shared goal with benefits in it for all, and a process of collaboration to achieve that goal. The board approved the alternative plan that the management and union presented together. The picture changed completely. The sailors and officers of this sinking ship, though wary of each other, stopped wrestling with each other and got down to fixing the ship together. Performance improvement accelerated and the plants were saved, along with many jobs and reputations.

The consultants left behind volumes of reports with detailed plans and projections of operating and financial results. But these would have been worth nothing if the spirit of collaboration and hope had not been kindled. A union leader said at a party given to thank the consultants. that the consultants' main contribution was not these reports, but the change they had brought about in the orientation of the people by listening to their hopes and fears, the development of a shared goal with benefits for all, and a fair process of give-and-take collaboration.

Returning home to Lexington that weekend, I felt more secure about what I could contribute to an American company with my experience with people in India. I realised that people everywhere have fears and hopes, whether they are Americans or Indians. And people everywhere can get locked into adversarial competition, when by collaboration they could create a better future for all. I realised that my best contribution as a consultant may be in my skills to help people work together.

I remembered the chairman of the Tata Administrative Services selection panel, Professor Choksi, asking me towards the end of the three-day selection process, way back in 1964, whether I had considered working in personnel (a function he led at Tatas). I was surprised because I had a master's degree in physics that seemed as far from personnel as anything I could imagine. Why would he even consider me qualified for personnel management? I inquired. He explained that the panel observed during the selection process that I was helping others to be heard and get their points understood, just as much as I concentrated on what I wanted to say. However, he changed the subject quickly when he realised that I seemed offended to even be considered a personnel type! Little did I realise then that the key to make change happen rather than merely be written about is the motivation of people, rather than analysis and plans. And that to be a successful executive, I would have to master the art of working with people.

Why does culture change have to take so long?

My next consulting project was in Mexico with a cement company. Cementos Mexicana (Cemex, for short) is the third largest and most profitable international cement company in the world today. However, when Cemex engaged Arthur D. Little in the early 1990s, Cemex was only a local Mexican company, fearful of the larger international companies that were entering the Mexican market. Moreover, the North American Free Trade Agreement (NAFTA) had been announced removing trade barriers between Mexico and the USA, allowing more competition from across the border. Cemex's CEO

Lorenzo Zambrano's concern was, what needed to be done to prepare the company for the much tougher international competition that was imminent. This is where the consultant's role came in.

Cemex was a very successful company in Mexico. The largest cement company in the country, the second largest corporation, and perhaps amongst the two or three most admired companies in Mexico. The winds of international competition could stir concern in the mind of Zambrano. But to people within the company, especially in cement plants in remote areas of the country, life seemed just fine. The company was very profitable. And they were making continuous improvements. Why worry? The consultants were asked to make an assessment of the gap between Cemex's productivity and costs and the best standards in the world and identify areas for improvement in Cemex.

Zambrano listened to the consultants' diagnosis. It was a well-documented account of the gaps in standards of kiln utilisation, energy consumption, workmen productivity, equipment turnaround time, and other performance parameters. The consultants also presented an impressive list of areas for improvements. But less than halfway through the presentation, Zambrano called for a halt. 'Why have these improvements not occurred to my people in the plants?' he asked. 'Why are they not doing something about these gaps?' With these questions he shifted the discussion from technology towards people. The consultant, a brilliant manufacturing engineer, was stumped. He replied that the problem was the 'culture' in the plants and the culture would have to be changed.

'Ah yes,' sighed Zambrano, 'I have heard about that problem from all the consultants that have studied our operations. They all say that the culture has to be changed. They also tell me that changing culture is difficult and takes a long time. But tell me this,' he said to the consultant, 'Why does culture change *have* to take so long? If everything is a process, as you suggest, and the performance of processes can be dramatically altered by "process engineering", which is your speciality, then why cannot the process of culture change be improved to reduce the time required to change culture? You say that process improvement has reduced the time for new product development, and time for service order fulfilment dramatically in many industries. Why cannot we similarly master and improve the process of culture change?'

Another member of our consulting team took up Zambrano's question. He said the problem of changing the culture of a large organisation was like inducing an elephant to make a U-turn. There was no use trying to force the elephant to turn: it was too big. The elephant will make a turn only when it wants to. He said that perhaps culture change would be faster if people wanted to change their own behaviours rather than being beaten on their heads to change. Zambrano was amused by the analogy. The idea that process improvement produces results was the rage in business circles at that time. Michael Hammer's book, *Reengineering the Corporation* and George Stalk's *Time Based Competition* were best sellers. I acknowledged the power of these ideas but have always maintained that processes do not change themselves alone. I pointed out that it is the thoughts and actions of people that make processes change. Therefore, a complete description of a manufacturing plant must include a picture of the people who work in it along with the map of the processes. In other words, a manufacturing plant, or any business organisation for that matter, must be seen as a 'socio-technical' system—a closely interwoven system of people and processes.

Zambrano saw merit in the discussion and commissioned our team to work in the Cemex plants to induce the radical improvements required to face the world's toughest competition. However, he imposed one condition on us. It was that the consultants must discover the critical factors that accelerate changes in culture and should document a process that Cemex could use thereafter without the assistance of consultants. To his mind, the ability of Cemex to learn and change faster than any potential competitor would be its source of sustainable competitive advantage.

Cemex had about a dozen plants in Mexico. We began our work in two plants, applying the best ideas we could find in the world to accelerate culture change and performance improvement. Using a comprehensive socio-technical model of the plants, rather than just the technical process maps, we applied ourselves to the leverage points for starting and accelerating change. We knew that these would be in the hopes and fears of people. Therefore, we engaged people with the questions, 'Why change now, when Cemex seems to be doing alright?' And, 'What would be their vision of Cemex which would give people benefits they aspired to have?'

When people thought of the benefits they could obtain, they applied themselves more vigorously to rethinking and changing work processes. As a result of this rethinking and innovation with work processes, performance improved. As the change progressed, we reviewed what had contributed to accelerate change and what apparently had not. These learnings were applied to the next few plants. The change in these plants was much faster. Once again we distilled our learnings and applied them to a further set of plants. Through this process of learning through action about how culture and performance change could be accelerated, we reduced the time required to a third of the original deadline and of course, with less effort. Zambrano was pleased with the changes he observed both in culture and performance at the plants. This exercise also provided Cemex with a documented process for accelerating change in socio-technical systems that could be used when it acquired plants in other countries as it began to expand internationally.

Embracing the human face of change

What I learned at Cemex was in many ways not anything new. My 25 years of experience with the Tatas, and the wisdom of JRD Tata and Sumant Moolgaokar had taught me that people are the only 'appreciating assets' in a business where machines may depreciate in value and knowledge may get outdated, but people can always learn and improve their own capabilities, and consequently improve performance and create knowledge. This insight had already enabled me to produce outstanding results for two clients. Perhaps I had found the answer to my question about how I, a middle-aged Indian executive without a management degree, could add value to clients in America. Moreover, my consulting team had developed capabilities to help clients accelerate performance improvement. What I needed now was the best tools for my team to systematically apply our insights and build a healthy consulting practice.

I found that the concepts and techniques of organisational learning provided many useful ideas. I worked very closely with Innovation Associates, a boutique consulting firm founded by Charlie Kiefer and Peter Senge, author of *The Fifth Discipline: The Art and Practice of the Learning Organisation*. In fact, I managed the firm for a while when it was acquired by Arthur D Little Inc. I also participated in a research project with Professor David Garvin of the Harvard Business School to study the many approaches to organisational learning that had been developed by academicians and consultants and find the best insights in the subject. Alongside, I continued to test these ideas with organisations with whom I consulted. Thus I distilled a framework for accelerating learning and change in organisations that I called the Learning Field.

In 1996, I wrote a book with a colleague, Dr Peter Scott-Morgan, describing a process and techniques for accelerating learning and change in organisations. Since we both believed that people were the only appreciating assets in an organisation, and were at the heart of change, the title of the book, appropriately was *The Accelerating Organization: Embracing the Human Face of Change.* In this book, I first described the process which I have continued to develop since, and of which I will write in detail later.

This book came into the hands of U Sunderajan, Chairman of Bharat Petroleum Corporation Ltd (BPCL), a public sector company in India. He had been mulling over what the future of his company would be in the more competitive environment that he anticipated following the liberalisation of the Indian economy. He aspired to make BPCL a customer-focussed, learning organisation. He liked what he read in my book and asked me to help him and his team to rethink the strategy of the company and reshape the organisation and its capabilities to achieve their vision. However, he had one non-negotiable condition: I would have to ensure that the process to make change faster would be transferred from the consultants to his people. And so a dozen certified 'master coaches' were trained in the company as the change process progressed. BPCL transformed its culture and improved its performance substantially and even won international awards for its innovations in accelerating performance improvement through people.

When I had left India for the USA in 1989, JRD Tata had suggested that I should learn something that would be useful for companies in India. However, when in the USA, I agonised about what I could contribute to my clients in America. In time I discovered that my experience with the Tatas had given me insights and skills that were useful and applicable everywhere. In the USA I found a community of intellectual partners and like-minded practitioners with whom I learned and developed sound concepts and tools.

Yet, I strongly felt there was something missing. Although my focus and my experiences had been change in business organisations, I was curious about how these principles and tools would apply to larger systems of people, like countries. I strongly felt that this could be a tremendous enabler. Through friends in the Global Business Network, which specialises in scenario planning, I met Adam Kahane. Adam, while he was with the scenario planning group in Royal Dutch Shell was invited to South Africa in the early 1990s, when the country was being torn apart by apartheid. Scenario planning was a technique that had been used by the Royal Dutch Shell Oil Company to foresee major developments in the environment which could affect their business strategy. Adam worked with a group of political leaders from different parties, business leaders, and others to apply the techniques of scenario thinking to get insights into what would be required to take South Africa onto a new trajectory of hope and progress. The Mont Fleur Project, as it was called, produced four alternative scenarios for South Africa. It also identified the principal driving forces that could produce the outcome that all the parties desired. Adam generously shared with me insights into principles and techniques from his work in South Africa as well as similar work he subsequently did in Canada, Colombia, and Guatemala.

After the initial surge of enthusiasm and change with the liberalisation of the economy in 1991, India seemed to be floundering in 1998. There was talk about the need for 'second generation' reforms, more complicated than the first wave, that had basically focussed on issues that affected business. The reforms now required would affect issues of labour laws, subsidies to farmers, and prices for power and utilities charged to consumers. These reforms would affect a much larger and more diverse set of stakeholders than the first round. It was not enough to have a plan. The plan would have to be implemented through a difficult political process.

As someone who had been watching the change process in India very closely, I was concerned that it should not lose its pace or direction. This led me to write to two old friends in

India, Dr Montek Singh Ahluwalia and Tarun Das. Dr Ahluwalia as a former Secretary for Finance in the Indian government had been a key member of the team that worked with the architect of the liberalisation process, Dr Manmohan Singh, then Finance Minister. Montek had moved to the Planning Commission. Tarun Das, Director General, CII had played an important role in working with the government to steer the reforms. Knowing that both cared deeply about the development of the country, I asked them whether they shared my feeling that the change process in India seemed to have been bogged down. I also asked whether they would like to consider approaches to accelerate change that seemed to have worked elsewhere. Both were intrigued by what I described and agreed to support an experimental process to try new techniques in India.

The process unfolded over the following eight months. It was anchored in three workshops. Several task forces were set up and explored subjects they considered most pertinent to the development of India. Over a 100 people participated in the process, ranging from children who lived on the streets outside Paharganj railway station in Delhi to senior bureaucrats. This diverse group of people expressed their aspirations for India and explored subjects that mattered to them. Insights were obtained by examining these subjects, such as education and governance, from different perspectives. A summary of this process was published by CII in a brief document titled *Scenarios for India 2010: Putting it Together Again.* The conclusion of the participants was that the process of participation worked and should be applied on a larger scale in the country. It would contribute to creating alignment amongst diverse people and renew the momentum for ·change towards an aspirational vision. This is critical because the only way India can achieve its much needed growth and development is by a participative process for arriving at a vision and its implementation.

My second book, *Shaping the Future: Aspirational Leadership in India and Beyond,* developed the insights from this experience and suggested how the concepts underlying the Learning Field could be extended to larger social systems, and to India in particular.

Coming home

The late 1990s were heady days in the USA. US style capitalism was ascendant everywhere. The Internet and the 'new economy' were creating excitement in business. The Soviet Union had crumbled. It was the triumph of US ideas, and the end of the history of conflicting ideologies, in Francis Fukuyama's famous expression. The mood in America was: the US had triumphed morally and was clearly the best. All other countries were either second best or still further behind.

Meanwhile, change in India accelerated in the 1990s. American, European, Japanese and Korean companies entered the Indian market to cater to the pent-up demand for better products of a growing middle-class estimated to be more than 100 million consumers: for TVs, air-conditioners, fast foods, and cars. Indian companies were finally relieved of the shackles of licensing. They no longer had to run to bureaucrats for permission to produce new products. Indians could now buy cars made by Daewoo, Honda, Fiat, Mercedes, General Motors, and Toyota, as well as a car designed and made by Telco—the Indica. While Indians, as consumers relished the choice of international cars available to them at last; Indians, as citizens were also proud of their own Indian company's daring to take on the world's best manufacturers with a product designed and made by Indians.

Though I lived in the US, my work brought me back to India regularly and I could feel the change in both countries. India was joining the capitalist world. It was OK to make money. Businessmen were now respected and business magazines,

newspapers and television channels had proliferated. Meanwhile, ·
the USA seemed to be moving into a new era of capitalism,
shedding the rules of the old economy for a new economy
whose ingredients were the Internet, information technology,
Silicon Valley, venture capitalists, and booming stock markets.
If making money was becoming fashionable in India, making
huge amounts of money without even making or selling
anything seemed to be the trend in the USA. Living there, as
I was, one sensed an arrogance in many Americans that they
had left the rest of the world, even Europe and Japan, way
behind. Obviously, India was not even in the reckoning.

At such a time India surprised the world by testing a nuclear
device in Pokhran. The criticism of India that I heard from my
American acquaintances was very sharp. They either implied or
even said outright that India was irresponsible and untrustworthy.
Irresponsible because India was a poor country that surely had
better uses for its limited resources than to build nuclear
weapons. And since it was dangerous for too many countries to
have nuclear weapons, it was best to leave them in the hands
of only those who could be trusted to use them wisely. There
seemed to be no doubt in the minds of these people that the
USA, even though it was the only country that had actually
used nuclear devices on civilian populations to devastating
effect, was the most trustworthy country. On the other hand,
India was still economically underdeveloped and therefore, by
implication, not mature enough to be trusted. This insinuation
rankled me and led to some sharp arguments.

Observing me in one of these discussions, an American
colleague noted my struggle to balance on the fine line between
acknowledging India's need to change in many ways to become
a better country for all its people, and yet demanding respect
for India's ideals and aspirations. What came through, she
observed, was that I cared deeply about India. And she asked
why I was in the USA offering my skills to organisations there
to achieve their goals when my heart was clearly in India.

My life in the USA was very comfortable. I enjoyed my work and was respected both in my consulting firm and by my clients as a senior thought-leader. My wife and I lived in a lovely area in Massachusetts where she kept a beautiful garden, and also learned to produce wonderful ceramics from a Japanese potter. On weekends, I would go for very long runs, and longer mountain-bike rides, into the woods, by streams, and over hills. There was peace, and I even wrote poetry! But my personal learning journey outside India had to end. The children were grown up and it was time to return. And so my wife, Shama, and I took the third turn in the road and came back to India in January 2000.

When we left the USA, the country was in a frenzy of 'irrational exuberance' in Alan Greenspan's words. It was the height of the boom of the 'new economy'. The bubble was yet to burst. And very few people in the USA or India thought it was likely to because they were being led to believe that the new economy did not work to the old rules. They were repeatedly reminded that Moore's Law of diminishing costs with enhanced capabilities continued to operate in the computer industry. Brian Arthur, the Nobel Prize winning economist suggested that the hoary old law in economics of diminishing returns on incremental investments no longer applied, and that the information economy operated on the principle of appreciating returns. Moreover, the advent of the Internet had 'blown to bits' old compromises in business, according to a best selling book with that eponymous title.

The Indian stock market was also booming, fuelled by the growth of Indian IT companies. Their returns were enormous and their growth prospects seemed unlimited because they were providing inexpensive, high quality manpower to companies in the USA which were investing heavily in new IT systems without which, they were led to believe, they could not survive in the new millennium.

The concept of a new economy flowed into business circles

everywhere, and Silicon Valley was the fountainhead. India was changing, but was yet a backwater. Students from the Indian Institutes of Management (IIMs), IITs, and other engineering colleges headed West. Young Indians, and even some older ones, were rushing to the USA to participate in the excitement. 'When so many people are wanting to go to the USA, why had we come back to India?' was a question many people wanted to ask my wife and me, and those who felt they could take the liberty, did. To some of them I could explain my motivation, which I have shared with the readers of this book. But many asked the question rhetorically. They did not wait for an answer but proceeded to tell us how they would rather be in the USA if they could.

However, the question we were asked most frequently was, 'What change do you notice in India since you left a decade back?' And those who asked this question were invariably interested in our answer.

We lived in the Taj Mahal hotel in Mumbai for the first six months until an apartment became vacant for us. In the evening, we would switch on the TV in our room and surf dozens of channels, even watch international shows, whereas in the 1980s we could only have watched government broadcasts in India. In fact we seemed to have a greater choice of channels in India than we had had in the USA! My wife commented on the changes in the social mores. For example, young Gujarati girls walking around late in the evenings in the hotel lobby were mostly wearing miniskirts and skimpy blouses. Hardly any girls wore the traditional Indian dresses that my wife was used to seeing when we lived in Mumbai earlier. In office, young men immediately called me by my first name, whereas I would have been addressed as 'Mr Maira' in the 1980s until I asked someone to call me 'Arun'. Clearly one noticeable change was the adoption of American ways of dressing and talking by the younger generation, influenced partly, no doubt, by what these youngsters were seeing on TV.

We could now smell money in the air! We heard that kids from schools in downtown Mumbai liked to show off the cars in which they were driven to school, the cellphones in their hands, and the hundreds of rupees in their pockets. Lunchtime conversation amongst young consultants in the office was very often about the stocks they were buying and how much money they had made (or lost). Some mainline newspapers devoted whole pages to pictures and snippets about rich people partying in their designer clothes, with champagne and whisky glasses in hand. There were rich people in India earlier as well. But had taken care to deodorise the smell of their money and not flaunt it as people were now doing.

Middle-class Indian consumers had many more things to buy now. We were impressed with the range of kitchen appliances, refrigerators, and home entertainment systems available in India. We could also see sleek Hondas, Mitsubishis, Hyundais, Mercedes and many other international brands parked on the road beneath our hotel window. This was a clear contrast from the 1980s when there were clunky Ambassadors and Padminis, and little Marutis, with perhaps an odd Mercedes amongst them.

We could also see a poor family living on the pavement amidst their meagre belongings. That had not changed. My office building at Nariman Point was surrounded by a slum, which had merely grown in size in the last 10 years. Whilst the smell of new money in the office and hotel was strong, the smell of poverty around such islands of wealth seemed even stronger than before.

I remember a conversation with another Indian couple who had also returned to the country after having stayed abroad for many years, and were staying temporarily in the Taj Mahal hotel. We compared notes on what struck us the most about the changes that had taken place in India whilst we were away. Surprisingly, we agreed it was the knocking on the windows of cars stopping at traffic lights! Mumbai always had beggars. But hardly any cars were air-conditioned in the 1980s, so people would drive with the windows rolled down. Therefore beggars could talk and plead with the occupants of cars when they stopped at the lights. Now the beggars were shut out. And they had to knock hard on the windows to attract the attention of the rich people enjoying their new comforts with the liberalisation of the Indian economy.

While Indians seemed inured to the poverty around them, and always had been, some foreigners were moved to help the poor families on the streets. Two European families staying at the Taj shared their dismay with us. They didn't even know what help the poor families would appreciate. One German kid had been moved to give some of his toys to the little beggar children swarming around his mother on the pavement outside the hotel, only to find that the toys promptly disappeared—perhaps sold immediately to get money to buy the more necessary objects for the family's subsistence. The other family bought cartons of milk, which they considered more essential than toys for kids, from the store behind the hotel and gave them to the children. They were shocked to find the children scoot with the cartons to the store and return with money in their hands!

From this kaleidoscope of impressions of change with the opening of the Indian economy emerged a concern. *When would the liberalisation of the economy benefit the poor people of India?* The economy had grown by an average of 5.7 per cent per annum during the 1990s. The number of people living below the poverty line had reduced from 39 per cent of the population in 1988 to 27 per cent in 2000. And literacy rates had increased from 52 per cent to 65 per cent between 1991 and 2001. It seemed the benefits of development and growth were flowing down to the poor. But since the Indian population had increased from 846 million to 1027 million in one decade, the absolute number of the illiterate and poor in the country remained very large. Unemployment remained very high—approximately 35 million people were recorded as unemployed, though economists said the actual number would be much higher, as it was not easy to count the unemployed in a country as vast as India. Some economists calculated that the Indian economy must grow at 9 to 10 per cent per year to ensure that the rate of creation of new jobs would keep pace with the growth of the population, which was much higher than the rate so far. Millions of poor people were waiting for better times, jobs, a decent shelter, and for things that they could see others around them afford. The moral question was: How long *should* they be patient? And the political question was: How long *would* they?

The first round of reforms in the early 1990s had removed the protective ring around Indian businesses and exposed them to a competitive market. It also began to get government out of the way of private business. According to economists what was now required was a second generation of reforms to dismantle public sector enterprises and reduce subsidies on commodities and services that distorted market prices. This second generation of reforms would remove the protective ring around people, especially poorer people. Politically these were more difficult in a democracy than the earlier round of reforms.

Meanwhile the 'bulls from the China shop' were ravaging India. Economists compared the huge flow of Foreign Direct Investment (FDI) into China with the relative trickle into India— $40 billion versus only $2 billion. The Indian government was taking a beating, at conferences and in the media, from Western and Indian businessmen for its tardiness with reforms. Why couldn't India be more like China, they all seemed to ask?

There are fashions in clothes, and also fashions in ideologies. Fashions in both were flowing much more strongly from the USA to India (and the rest of the world) than they had done a few years earlier. We noticed the rage of American fashion in clothes worn by young people. Similarly, business was moving towards the American style of shareholder capitalism rather than European stakeholder capitalism to which Indian business had been ideologically closer. And in economics' circles, market-based capitalism, favoured by Wall Street, was clearly dominant. The economist Hy Minsky had said that there are as many types of capitalism as there are varieties of Heinz pickles. In 2000, one variety of capitalism, the only one popular in the USA, seemed to be in high fashion in India.

Solutions to India's problems of slow growth seemed obvious to businessmen and to the Indian and American economists who were in fashion. The only problem they said was that the government lacked the will. The tragedy of India, these pundits said, was coalition politics. Prime Minister Vajpayee was criticised for being too concerned with building a consensus. All that was required they said, like the popular Nike slogan, was for the Indian government to 'Just Do It'. I respected the intelligence and was awed by the success of these people. I did not have an alternative prescription that I felt as confident about as they seemed about theirs. So I listened to them. But I was not easily convinced. If it were only so simple, I thought!

The lens through which I made sense of my swirling impressions of the forces of change in India were the concepts of organisational learning and change. Coming in from the outside, India seemed to be a society in search of a unifying and guiding idea. Socialism was no longer acceptable to most people. And whereas the US style of capitalism, and in particular the style of Wall Street capitalism, was in high fashion in some circles, it was a borrowed idea, and many were not sure it was appropriate for India at this stage of development. (Nor were many in the USA sure that it was the best idea for their society!) I was more curious about how the new idea for India would emerge rather than what it would be. Many people were concerned with the slackening of the pace of change that was getting mired in the conflicting interests of many political parties and sections of society. I wondered what process could align different views in a society as vast and as diversified as India, and whether that process of aligning goals while reaching out for the greatness that Indians aspired for could begin to provide the glue the Indian polity needed.

An Enterprise of People

The key to creating markets at the 'bottom of the pyramid' is to grow incomes of poor people in rural areas by making them part of extended, networked enterprises. Corporations should consider new models of organising and governing businesses; IT can be an enabler

T HE CEO of one of India's larger companies and I had both returned to India after a few years abroad. 'What is the change that is noticeable?' we asked each other one evening. 'The knocking on the window,' he said. There had always been poor people on the streets, and beggars. But one could have ignored them if one chose to. Now they knock hard on the windows of cars at traffic lights, and it is not easy to chase them away. The cars have changed too. Five years back, Ambassadors and Padminis chugged amongst the Marutis in the city traffic. Now they are almost gone. In their place, many more cars such as Hyundais, Fords, Daewoos, Hondas, Opels, and Mitsubishis swarm the roads. And the beggars knock on their windows.

Article first published in *The Economic Times.*

In India, as everywhere in the world today, leaders of business corporations must shoulder a greater responsibility for answering the knock on the window. Governments are being asked to downsize themselves, to step out of running businesses, and to hand over the running of public services to private managers. Government leaders consult with business leaders more closely than before and it has even become fashionable for heads of governments to call themselves CEOs, to suit the temper of our times! But prevalent models of business leadership cannot provide a sufficient response to the knocking that will get louder. Therefore, business leaders must discover new solutions that, while meeting the increasing demands of their own shareholders, also address broader social issues.

People want money to buy food, clothes and shelter and to buy toiletries, consumer durables, and the other products and goodies that corporations would hope they will buy. The poor people then must somehow earn this money. Putting them onto the bloated rolls of government departments and corporations is not a sustainable solution. Even private Indian companies have to improve their productivity substantially, and many need to shed people from their rolls and not take on more candidates. The wisdom of economics says that over a period of time, the improvement of efficiencies in the public and private sectors will make the economy more vibrant, and there will be a growth of incomes which will trickle down to the poorer people. However, the interim will be uncomfortable for CEOs. Morally, this discomfort will be heightened with the knocking on the window. And strategically insecure, because it is not clear how long the political system will be able to withstand the pressure and hold its course of privatisation and downsizing if it does not quickly produce strong evidence of the benefits of this course to the presently poor population.

Business leaders can overcome their moral discomfort by providing money to social causes. Better still, they can provide the time of their managers to help community efforts. Several Indian companies are doing exemplary work in this regard. However, these efforts may be insufficient to address the root cause of the problem. This is the need for people to see their own incomes rise quickly, along with the success of the business enterprises that the new economic policies are assisting. Therefore, we need a new model of business enterprise, with new approaches to production and distribution, in which poorer people are engaged in larger numbers as free agents rather than as employees of large corporations, whereby they earn and also contribute to the growth of the corporations.

Not only do emerging markets like India have a need for this new model of business organisation but businesses in Silicon Valley, arguably the richest place on the planet, also require reorganisation. There and elsewhere the excitement of the new economy has changed the nature of the relationship between people and corporations. The dot-com entrepreneurial spirit jives with neither corporate imperialism nor corporate paternalism. In the very rich countries it is the people who are becoming less enamoured with employment in corporations. Whereas in poor countries, corporations do not want more people on their payrolls but want that people should have incomes nevertheless. Either way one arrives at the same set of organisational issues. These are:

- How can you engage large numbers of people with your enterprise without putting them on your payroll?
- How can you ensure they will do their work diligently to meet the needs of your enterprise without a hierarchical edifice to coordinate their activities?
- How will people acquire the resources, skills and money they would need to play their roles?
- What will be the design of boundary-spanning business processes in such a networked enterprise?

- How will the value created be equitably shared between the many independent participants?
- Who will set the minimum critical rules that all members of such an enterprise must abide by for it to function coherently?

Answers to these questions are emerging. Some of the organisational innovations required can be found, at this time, outside traditional business organisations. Business innovation will happen when leaders take some well known ideas and some emerging ideas, adapt them, and create the missing pieces thus completing the bigger picture to make a new model work. Let us summarise some emerging solutions as well as some important issues that need to be addressed.

A new model for organising and governing

Advances in information and communication technologies along with the Internet have completely changed the way in which information can be exchanged and activities coordinated. It is no longer necessary to have a central coordinator to whom all information is passed and who processes it and passes back instructions. People can coordinate with each other directly. Until very recently, the belief was that people would need personal computers (PCs) to participate in such networks and therefore the poor people in India would have to be excluded. But the continuing ferment of technologies as well as innovations in business models for providing access to people who do not own communication devices will soon overcome this limitation.

It is no longer necessary for people to belong to a large corporation to obtain access to customers, suppliers, and providers of capital. A host of new businesses have emerged to meet the needs of entrepreneurs. These range from venture capitalists to micro-lending schemes; online and offline training programmes; and providers of logistical services. With these possibilities, corporations do not themselves have to provide or even pay for the resources they need for their enterprise.

Relations between the multiple parties in these web-like networks can function on commercial terms rather than as charity. Even the poor will honour their debts so long as the terms of the contracts are fair. Underprivileged women and children have shown themselves to be very reliable business partners. The success of the Grameen Bank in micro lending to women is well known. However, what is lesser known is the success of a scheme of lending to street children in Mumbai. These children, who do not even have an address, are taught a trade and then lent money to start up a micro venture such as selling flowers. The only security the child is required to provide is a photograph and a surety from two friends, who are invariably also homeless street children. Remarkably, the recovery of these loans, from the poorest of the poor, has been over 75 per cent!

The governance of networked enterprises of small and large businesses and the management of twentieth century, monolithic companies require different concepts and skills. In the former, stakeholders are more diffused and the power of ownership and positional authority cannot be wielded to obtain control. The core curriculum of management education and practice so far has been focussed on the management of traditional business corporations. This curriculum has shaped the lenses managers use through which they distinguish the interesting opportunity from the pie-in-the-sky, because the assessment of opportunity is inevitably closely related to the know-how managers have in order to make certain types of things take place.

The major obstacles to producing the organisational innovation we need could be our thinking. As Einstein said, 'The significant problems we face cannot be solved at the same level of thinking that we were at when we created them.' Extended enterprises in which the poor earn and so are able to spend may well be dismissed as utopian. One can imagine all kinds of problems. However, many things that were considered impossible or stupid at some time have now come to pass. For example, Watson of IBM, and later Olson of Digital, grandly misjudged what the future shape of the computer industry would be. And it is not only Watson and Olson, but also many other successful people in different fields who have failed to anticipate innovations. Experts can become constrained by the lenses they use to look at the world around themselves. Whereas if they can use another lens, they may see a different world already emerging—which they may even take the lead in the formation of, rather than be overtaken by.

Indian business leaders will need a new approach to increase the purchasing power of the poor more quickly. Not only so that the poor can afford to buy what corporations seem to try and sell to them but also to answer that knocking on the window. There is no management textbook to provide us the solutions, certainly not in the richer countries, because this is an urgent problem for business leaders in poor yet democratic countries such as India. The leaders in India will be those who experiment and discover pathways for accelerated development and growth of their businesses in India. The knocking on the window may not only be a warning, but an opportunity to grow our businesses as well. This is something we are unable to recognise through the management lenses we are presently wearing. If business leaders can now change their lenses by using other approaches for organising, such as organisational learning and scenario thinking, instead of analytical strategy and traditional organisational structures, they may discover new pathways into the future. These approaches have been used in the past decade by a few businesses, communities, and even countries such as South Africa, to create powerful visions of the future. More importantly, they enable better alignment amongst the diverse stakeholders of the future, whether they be rich or poor, on the political left or right, and black or white (as in the case of South Africa).

In Search of Excellence in India

Leaders can change the culture of shoddiness and 'chalta hai' that seems to pervade India by demanding excellence relentlessly. Indians can produce the best quality in the world

INDIA has aspirations to build world-class infrastructure in its cities, increase exports of manufactured goods manifold, and become the world's largest provider of skill-based services. However, the Achilles heel of these aspirations may very well be the subterranean culture of shoddiness that seems to pervade life in India. A carpenter leaves an uneven gap in the door. An electrician fixes a point crookedly in the wall. A plumber does not show up when he said he would. A painter does not clean up when his work is done. And a contractor excuses himself for poor quality because his subcontractors do not perform. These are people who do not take pride in their work. Sadly, we accept such ordinariness—*chalta hai*—in our daily lives. This is our culture, we say. And it is difficult to change, is our

---

Article first published in *The Economic Times*.

constant complaint. However, we could change it provided we want to and know how to go about making it happen.

The keys to excellence are, first to want it; second, expect people to deliver it; and third, if one is responsible for the work of others, to give them the tools to produce it. Several Indian manufacturing companies, using these keys, have demonstrated that Indians can produce the best quality in the world. Nevertheless, many Indian manufacturers have a long way to go still. And the drive for excellence must be extended vigorously to the infrastructure and basic service sectors as well. Therefore, let us understand how these keys to excellence work.

Sumant Moolgaokar of Telco had a dream to create a factory in Pune that would make Indians proud. Young engineers were compelled to learn new skills to produce complex machines that had never before been produced in India. I remember the pride with which I took him, in 1981, to the factory floor to see a massive machine designed and built for the first time in the country. Over 50 metres long, with many miles of electrical wire and hydraulic tubing, it automatically machined a casting fed at one end into a cylinder head at the other. Instead of being pleased, Moolgaokar was visibly disturbed when he saw the result of our year's effort! 'Look at the hydraulic pipes: they are not parallel to each other!' he said. 'Trifles make for perfection. And perfection is no trifle,' he added. The machine had to be redone. Because Moolgaokar was a man who wanted the best and was determined to get it. And his persistence enabled Indian engineers to show that they were inherently not less than the best engineers anywhere.

Moolgaokar, one of the country's greatest engineers, was striving for excellence. And so was Lakshman, a driver in Telco. I was barely 30 and Lakshman was almost 60 years old. Every time we arrived at a destination, he would run around the car to open the door for me. I suggested that I was young enough to do it myself. He said that it was not me that he was concerned about but the car! He did not want me to bang the door shut. He said he was striving to set a new standard for maintenance-free performance of Ambassador cars before he retired in a year's time. He was tracking the maintenance records of all the company cars. While all other cars had chalked up the usual high costs, costs for his car were negligible. What amazed me was that there was no scheme to hold drivers accountable for maintenance costs. Therefore, no one other than Lakshman even knew what he was striving for. He demonstrated to me, unforgettably, that pride in work and the pursuit of excellence are hardly the exclusive purview of the educated elite.

People want to do better. They want to be proud of themselves. The job of leaders is to provide them the tools to help them along. When all the workmen in Telco were introduced to Total Quality Management (TQM) in the early 1980s, the group that turned in the best improvements were the 'uneducated' canteen boys employed by a workmen's cooperative. They were not even part of the official TQM rollout. But they were thirsty to learn. They formed teams on their own, picked up the tools of TQM, and applied them to improve the customer experience in the canteens and reduce cost. Very soon the canteens were showpieces of whose standards Telco was as proud of as its machine shops. The canteen boys also won awards at inter-company TQM contests, competing against teams of engineers from other companies. Therefore let us not write off anyone as incapable of producing excellence. Not even the artisans and petty contractors with whose examples I began this article.

The Nobel Prize winning author, VS Naipaul, who had written off India in his books, *India: An Area of Darkness* and *India: A Wounded Civilization*, saw the seeds of a new India when he visited Pune. In his latter book he wrote with hope, 'The plateau around Pune is now in parts like a new country, a new continent ... (Telco managers and workers) say that they are building for the twenty-first century ... Men handling new machines, exercising technical skills that to them are new, can also discover themselves as men, as individuals.'

There are two lessons in these stories. The first, contrary to the views of some writers including Naipaul, is that there is nothing in the Indian character that dooms us to half-measures and slip-shod execution. If the workmen of TVS Motors, the staff of Jet Airways, and the canteen boys of Telco can do it, we need no more proof that Indians can achieve world-class standards in their work. Admittedly, these stories describe exceptions, and the general condition is sloppy. Something is required to spark a broader movement of change.

The second lesson in the stories is that there is a way to produce the change. Leaders change cultures towards excellence by setting high standards, expecting good performance from all people, giving them the tools they need, and never accepting less than the best. But since India is not Singapore, citizens cannot be fined by the state for being sloppy. We, the citizens and customers of services, will have to take it upon ourselves not to accept anything less than the best from each other. Each of us may be as guilty of failing to deliver the excellence that we are capable of as the others we accuse of falling short. Do we want excellence in India? It is in our hands.

3

Learning

Fields

Yes, a delegation going abroad on a study tour. He told the press that on reaching there, he would decide what they should study!

3

Learning Fields

Where the clear stream of reason has not lost its way
Into the dreary desert sand of dead habit . . .
Into that heaven of freedom, O Father,
Let my country awake

—Rabindranath Tagore, *Gitanjali*

THE forces that I see when I view the currents of change in Indian society are identified by the lens I use to see the reality. My point of view, as I have already admitted, is the perspective of organisational and societal learning. The lens, inside my head, is the framework of the Learning Field, which I will now briefly explain since the remainder of the book is organised accordingly.

The Learning Field, shown in Figure 3.1, is formed by combining two dimensions of learning. On one hand, we must understand 'who' is learning. Is it an individual or the organisation? Training programmes focus primarily on the knowledge and behaviour of individuals. But smarter individuals do not necessarily create better organisational performance. Team learning also plays a vital role in improving organisational performance as the Japanese have shown the world by implementing 'small group' level learning processes in many industries. However, ideas such as TQM and Just-in-Time (JIT) Manufacturing have to be learnt by the organisation's leaders and must be absorbed at an organisation-wide level to be effective. Thus learning at the individual, group, and organisational-wide levels interact with each other and must support each other for an organisation's culture to change and for its collective behaviour to be more intelligently directed towards its goals. To accelerate change, it is necessary to determine where the needs for intervention are. For example, more training of individuals, when the barriers to learning are at the level of organisational ideas, is not helpful and can even be counter-productive. This is because it can heighten the frustration of people who are learning new ideas with the organisation's leadership if changes required at an organisation-wide level are not simultaneously taking place.

Organisational learning is not merely the summation of the learning of all individuals in the organisation. The behaviour of an organisation as a whole is determined by a complex interaction amongst the individuals and groups in it. Therefore, the way people interact and the products of their interactions contribute to learning and change at the level of organisational culture and performance. Organisational learning is often left to chance, to happen on its own, stimulated by learning at the individual level. Alternatively, leaders of organisations may choose to understand how the interactions produce organisational learning and thereby accelerate change in the organisation.

The fourth column of the Learning Field recognises another class of learner: An entire society, or a network of organisations, that changes its guiding ideas and the ways in which it takes collective actions. There are several structural differences between organisations and societies, as indeed there are between organisations, individuals, and teams. Therefore processes for societal learning cannot be merely mechanically scaled-up versions of organisational-level learning processes. For example, one relevant structural difference between societies and business organisations is the difference in the source and nature of the power of leaders at the top over the organisation they lead. In business corporations the authority is granted by appointment from above. In democratic societies, it is granted by the people. Therefore CEOs in businesses can command and control more easily, with less concern for the effect of their actions, at least in the short term, on the people they lead so long as they produce long-term results, whereas leaders in democratic societies have to be much more skilful in the ways in which they carry people with them even in the short term, because they can otherwise very easily lose their mandate to lead. Hence political and societal leaders who take pleasure in calling themselves CEOs and allow their behaviour to slip into a CEO-like mode (sometimes assisted by business management consultants), lose touch with their political realities and are surprised when they are voted out of power even when they believe they were delivering great results.

Figure 3.1: The Learning Field*

What the Learning is about	Who is Learning			
	Individual	Team	Organisation	Society
Know-Wants (Aspirations/ Vision/Values)	What we Want			
Know-Whys ('Theories-in-use/Concepts')	What we Believe			
Know-How (Processes/ Structures)	What we Do			
Know-What (Information/ Procedures)	What we Hear/Say			

*Adapted to the terminology in this book.

The other, vertical dimension in the Learning Field builds on the insight that learning is not merely a cognitive activity. It also has emotional and aspirational sides to it. Peter Senge, author of *The Fifth Discipline*, and his colleagues at Innovation Associates with whom I worked very closely, made a significant contribution to my understanding of concepts and techniques of learning at the non-cognitive and emotional levels. Their research builds on the research of Robert Fritz and others who investigated the processes of creativity in the sciences, arts and business. It revealed that new ideas emerge from a state of 'creative tension' that is stimulated by an aspirational vision. 'Unlearning' of embedded beliefs and concepts, which is required to overcome resistance to change and make room for the testing of new concepts, can happen when there is a deeper and higher aspiration that cannot be fulfilled without letting go of these concepts. Therefore, the Learning Field gives a prominent place to the development of shared aspirations and values as a specific domain of organisational and societal learning.

The Learning Field also distinguishes three types, or levels, of cognitive learning. One is the knowledge of routines and data which is the scope of traditional 'knowledge management' systems. Another is the absorption of fundamental concepts, or 'theories-in-use' as Chris Argyris of Harvard calls them. In between the two lies the knowledge of principles that translate concepts (or 'theories') into practice and guide work routines and behaviours. Innovative strategies and transformational change in organisations invariably require learning at the level of new theories and new principles rather than merely new routines.

The four chapters that follow explain each of the four levels of learning through stories that bring out the power of the concepts, and articles that explain how the concepts relate to the process of change in India.

How to Accelerate from Zero to Sixty in Six Seconds

Reflections in February 2002 on the frenzy before the ritual of the national budget; the unrealistic expectation that the budget will bring about transformation of the country; and the need to look deeper for the real levers for change

T HE national budget season is a time for debates. Just now, the country's economic growth has slowed. The global economy is in a slump, but that should not significantly affect our growth, say many pundits: We have our own problems to solve. Problems related to bringing about change in several things including governance, regulations and the *chalta hai* culture. How much difference will the debates really make to the course of events? Quite little, our experience suggests.

When I lived in the USA I indulged myself with the fastest car I could buy, a BMW 3-series sports car. It could go from zero to sixty miles an hour in less than six seconds. The catch was it did not do this automatically. First, I had to buy a

Article first published in *The Economic Times*.

manual-shift version since the automatic-shift version was slower. Second, I had to learn how to move through the gears effectively to obtain the potential acceleration. I learned that to start from standstill, or when I approached a hill, I should downshift to a lower gear rather than merely pressing harder on the accelerator. That is how I would obtain the acceleration required.

I believe that if we want to accelerate change and growth in India, the time has come to take our conversations into the first and second gears, rather than pressing on at the level at which we are presently having the discussions about our future. A shared vision of the future is the equivalent of the first gear. The more passion there is for this vision, the more power there is in the process of change. We do not have a shared vision of what we would want India to be. Some of us want to be like China in some respects, but even these people do not want other features of Chinese polity. Others want to be like the USA, but again not in every way. A few cite Singapore as their model though they are also quick to admit that it cannot apply without modification that suits the context of India. What is the quality that we want our country to possess? What are the essential characteristics of this nation that we aspire to have? What is the place we want to occupy in the community of nations? The more this is a shared vision, the more we will align in our efforts to make the necessary changes. Shared visions cannot be created by presentations of numbers and intellectual debates. Nor are they shaped by political negotiations. They require deeper dialogues. Moreover, these dialogues must include the wants of diverse stakeholders of the country, rich and poor, north and south, among others.

Creating a shared vision is a first step but it alone is not enough. We have to move into the phase of the second gear. This is to challenge our underlying 'theories-in-use' to understand how we can accelerate change towards achieving our vision. It is widely accepted that two important areas in which we must implement better approaches are the governance of our large, democratic country, and the process of economic development. However, as I listen to the debates on these issues, I realise that deeper underlying beliefs shape the nature of the solutions that are being advocated. And it is the clash of these underlying beliefs that prevents alignment regarding solutions. For example, many have the belief that the only way that people can be made to change is through strong sticks along with economic carrots. This belief leads to a requirement of a strong, central authority as the means to produce change. However, others believe sticks and carrots only produce compliance and not commitment, and that transformational change requires commitment that comes from caring for a deeper cause. Their belief suggests that the process of change has to be built around the creation of shared visions and honest dialogues. These different beliefs suggest different approaches to the governance of large organisations and societies. Whatever may be our underlying beliefs, we have to find a solution that will work. Therefore we have to understand the reality in which our solution must apply. Maybe a strong central authority is a valid model in some situations and the approach of democratic dialogue is valid in others. An insightful examination of the key characteristics of our present reality may be a better way to come to an agreement about which is the best approach for our situation, rather than hurling examples at each other on the approaches that we intuitively favour.

From these two steps of 'Know-Want' and 'Know-Why', which are the first two gears to generate acceleration of change, we can step back into the third and fourth gears. These are the debates of the 'Hows' and 'Whats', viz. the regulations and policies that need to be changed. I fear that if we do not downshift the subjects as well as the mode of our national conversations to obtain deeper levels of alignment, we will not get the traction for faster change.

The Values We Choose to Live By

Entrepreneurship and pursuit of economic wealth are essential but will be insufficient to change India into a fully 'developed' country

Surfing through news channels and browsing through weekend newspapers in the USA in February 2004, I tapped into several interesting debates. These were the debates on who lied about WMD in Iraq, wartime service records of the presidential candidates, gay marriage, outsourcing, and other matters. However, the debate that set me thinking most was whether sportsmen should play for their country or for money. Because this led my mind to several questions about the values that are surfacing in American and even Indian society.

Professional sports are a big business in the USA. Teams have 'owners'. Players are paid enormous amounts of money, and are bought and traded like furniture. The owner of the Dallas Mavericks, a basketball team, has hired players from several countries. *The New York Times* reported that the owner

Article first published in *The Economic Times*.

was mad that his players were also playing for their own countries in international competitions. He said these additional games were tiring them, and since he was paying them, they had no business to waste their energy elsewhere. His point of view conforms to two underlying principles of market-based capitalism. One is, money counts. The other is, individuals must look after their own interests. There is nothing inherently wrong with either of the two principles. But both can be stretched too far.

A welcome change in Indian society in the 1990s was that it became respectable to make and have money. When I moved to the USA just before the liberalisation of the Indian economy, I had hardly any money. An American colleague asked me quite bluntly, 'If you don't have any money, how can you be any good?' Because money was the only measure he understood of a person's worth. Money is an easy measure because it is quantifiable. But if money becomes the only measure of value, we will lose sight of values that cannot, and perhaps should not, be monetised. If sportsmen were to believe, as the owner of the Dallas Mavericks suggests, that money is all that they should play for, loyalty to team and country would disappear. Going further, sportsmen could even believe that the aim should be to lose so long as there is more money to be made that way! Which may explain the temptations to fix matches that some sportsmen have succumbed to. Maybe it is time to rewrite the lesson of sports we were taught at school. It should now say, 'When the one great writer comes to write against your name, he will ask not whether you won or lost but how much money you made in the game!'

In February 2004, I also heard Dr Bimal Jalan, former Governor of the Reserve Bank of India (RBI), speak about JRD Tata, the only businessman to be conferred with the Bharat Ratna, India's highest civilian honour. He said JRD was special because whenever there was a trade-off, he always put the interests of society and the nation ahead of the interests of his own companies. JRD's values would be anathema to economists like Milton Friedman who say that the business of business must only be business, and to those management consultants and business analysts who expect business leaders to focus single-mindedly on producing money for their own shareholders. JRD Tata's concern for small shareholders was legendary. And his striving for excellence in the businesses he ran, such as Air India and Tata Steel, made the nation proud. His greatness lay in simultaneously keeping two goals in sight—the goal of business and the broader goals of society.

The contrast in the ways two diverging schools of thought interpret the concept of value is stark. One school's proponents, like the owner of the Dallas Mavericks, and many business analysts and economists appear to value materialism above all else, and seem willing to sacrifice almost anything to generate profits. For the other school that Dr Jalan was alluding to, value means more than what can be measured in terms of money. The former is generally associated with modern, Western, and particularly American values while the latter is often dismissed as being old-fashioned and 'anti-progress'.

There is a chauvinistic yearning in our country to call upon the values from our own heritage to guide our development; perhaps to moderate the greed and selfishness engendered by unalloyed market-based capitalism. Many are searching our ancient texts for these values. Let me recommend two. I learned these in my Indian school and from my Indian managers at the Tatas. Therefore I consider these as Indian, whether or not they are explicitly mentioned in our scriptures. The first value is the respect for common property, such as public spaces and the environment.

I was at the Goa airport some months back. The lounge was full of people puffing away even though there was a huge sign saying, 'No Smoking'. A lady sitting beside me went up to two foreigners who were smoking and pointed out the sign to them. They commented that many people were smoking around the area. However, they reluctantly stubbed out their cigarettes. That encouraged the lady to go to two well-dressed (and I am sure even 'foreign educated') Indians and point out the sign to them. They were affronted and said, 'Mind your own business.' Standing in the long immigration lines at Sahar airport, I always find many staff rushing through with 'important' Indian people while ordinary citizens are expected to wait in queues. Such incidents make me ask: For whom are the rules made; for whom are the systems established; and to whom does the environment we all share belong? I suppose the answer to all these questions is, 'everyone'. The hypocrisy is that those who complain about India being dirty and disorganised are invariably those who feel they are above the rules and who jump the queues with impunity. In their minds, the rules and the systems are there to discipline the rest.

It is not an uncommon practice in India to keep spotlessly clean houses and to dump one's trash out onto the street, and then complain about unclean public places! I have always wondered why the exteriors of buildings in Mumbai look so shabby. I often thought that perhaps it is the tropical climate. But then I could not understand why buildings in other tropical cities, like Singapore, did not look so bad. The CEO of one of India's most successful paint companies solved the riddle for me. He said his company was doing very well with expensive interior paints and had given up pushing high quality exterior paints in Mumbai. The reason is, he said, 'People, especially the very rich, put all their money into doing up their own flats. But they do not want to spend on the maintenance of exteriors which are common property.'

Though we want a country that functions more effectively, there is a gross selfishness in the air. On the economic front, we want the government to get out of the way, and unshackle the spirit of individuals and businesses to make profit and create wealth. I subscribe to that freedom wholeheartedly. But

I also ask will that by itself make India a better country: Cleaner, more orderly and safer for all? The answer is no. Because neither do we have the capability in our government nor do we have role models, especially amongst our better educated and wealthier people, who demonstrate by their actions their respect for public systems even when it is personally inconvenient.

The second value is to use the power that comes with position or wealth to help those who are weak, rather than to procure benefits for oneself and one's friends. Democratic societies cannot be strong if people cannot trust those with power in the system, whether they are politicians or businessmen, to look beyond their own petty interests. I do not need to give examples to illustrate how much this value has broken down in our society. People are dismayed by the selfishness and corruption of people with power and wealth.

We need role models. For me, JRD Tata was a great role model. He was at the apex of the largest business group in India. Yet he lived simply. And the humblest people, within the Tata organisation and outside, knew they could rely on him to uphold their interests. But another role model who had an equally profound effect on me was my house prefect in my boarding school. Though physically small, he vigorously used his position to stop bigger boys from bullying little fellows. In school, I also learned that I must pick up any scrap of paper even if I had not dropped it, to make the school cleaner for everyone. And this value was reinforced for me during my time with the Tatas, where not only the factories themselves, but the environment around the factories had to be improved and enriched.

These values can be learned through the examples of role models, and through practice in school and work. I would recommend that such values be at the core of 'value-based' education in India because they will propel us towards realising our vision of becoming a developed country.

4

Crises of

Aspiration

All the time you ask for drinking water. Don't you ever want to progress? I'm telling you I'm giving you telephones.

4

Crises of Aspiration

'Only where love and need are one,'
And work is play for mortal stakes,
Is the deed ever really done,
For Heaven and the future' sakes

—Robert Frost, 'Two Tramps in Mud Time'

The learning factory

WHEN I was with the Tatas, Sumant Moolgaokar, CEO of Telco, often referred to the new factory in Pune as a 'learning factory'. Telco was allotted about a 1000 acres of completely barren, stony land at Pimpri, some miles from Pune, in a new industrial area which the Maharashtra government had planned to develop. Here Telco would build its new factory to design and manufacture commercial vehicles and later cars, without the support of its former technical collaborator and teacher, Daimler Benz. The first programmes Moolgaokar commissioned were a massive tree-planting campaign and the creation of a training school. In the early years, the signs of young life and growth that a visitor to the factory at Pimpri would see, were hundreds and thousands of tree saplings and hundreds of young apprentices amidst factory buildings under construction. Moolgaokar often said that of all the renewable resources required by man, the two that take the longest to develop are a stand of timber and a body of trained manpower. Therefore he started with them.

The tree-planting programme turned out to be much harder than he had imagined. But ways were found to overcome the problems. The land was mostly stone and nothing would grow on it. So hundreds of thousands of pits were dug and filled with soil. There was no water for the trees. In fact there was precious little for the factories and homes that were coming up in the new industrial area the government was developing. Therefore, the company was forbidden to use any of the scarce government water for tree-planting activities. Telco invited water diviners, some from as far as Australia, to find water beneath the company's own land. However, all these efforts were fruitless and no water was found.

Nevertheless, persistence did yield a solution. A study of the topography of the company's large tract of land revealed the possibility of catching the water runoff from the land if a dam were to be built at one end. So a dam was constructed. Behind it grew a lake, from which water was drawn for the trees. Dr Salim Ali, the world-renowned ornithologist advised Moolgaokar to plant special grasses and weeds around the lake that would create a habitat for water birds to nest. As they grew, and birds came, the lake became a beautiful bird sanctuary to which migratory geese from Siberia would also come in the winters. The idea of a bird sanctuary abutting the walls of a big, busy factory seemed far-fetched, but it came about.

Trees take long to grow, and so do skilled people, as Moolgaokar noted. He urged his managers to find ways to accelerate both processes. He found a horticulturist, MD Sharma, who was an experimenter and innovator. Sharma found ideas from all over the world and developed some of his own. It was not too long before the barren land was a forest of flowering trees that inspired many other industries around, and even the government to adopt these techniques to change their surroundings. It seemed that not only Telco, but also the community around it was learning new ways with which to create the environment it wanted to live in.

In 1971, I was working in Mumbai as Moolgaokar's Executive Assistant with two assignments—devising a plan to accelerate the development of the manpower Telco needed for its growth, and assisting Moolgaokar with the plans for the Pune factory. The same year a crisis arose at Pune when the General Manager of the factory, a hard-driving man, who was pushing himself and the people around him relentlessly, had a heart attack. He was out of commission at a very critical time. In his absence, Moolgaokar decided that I must proceed to Pune immediately as the acting General Manager.

I was 28 years old and I had no experience of managing a factory. The three Deputy General Managers and several Divisional Managers in Pune were much older than me. They were seasoned technical people who had learned their crafts in Jamshedpur with Daimler Benz, and had been hand-picked to build the new Pune factory. They were an outspoken lot who usually expressed their views strongly. They expected that one of them would be given the chance to take charge. I was sure they would not accept a young novice as their boss, even temporarily, and I did not look forward to my encounters with them.

I shared with Moolgaokar my feeling of inadequacy and apprehension of the unpleasant reception I would get from these senior people. Moolgaokar was always a man of few words. All he said to me was, 'You do not have to impress them. Let them impress you. Go to Pune not to instruct, but to learn.'

Learning in the line of fire is perhaps the best way to learn. The apprehension of failing to achieve goals that really matter creates emotional and cognitive tension. This tension spurs the willingness to consider new ways and ideas with which the goals can be achieved. In their book, *Geeks and Geezers: How Era, Values, and Defining Moments Shape Leaders*, Warren Bennis and Robert Thomas report their research into the conditions that shape leaders. They interviewed both young and old leaders (hence the title of the book) from diverse walks of life. They found two essential conditions in the histories of all these leaders. One was their orientation to always learn from whatever they were doing. The other necessary condition was what they called a 'crucible', which was a crisis that tested them and strengthened them. They found that many people have similar crises in their lives. What distinguished the leaders was that they used these tough times to discover new ideas, new skills, and new strengths, whereas other people would get crushed.

One of my favourite expressions of this tension that shapes leaders is in the words of Alexander the Great. When he was growing up, he had the ambition of conquering the world. The rest as they say is history. Alexander went on to defeat the mighty Persian empire and the armies of Porus in India. He said to his biographer, Eumenes, 'The Gods put dreams in the hearts of men—dreams, desires, aspirations that are often much bigger than they are. The greatness of a man corresponds to that painful discrepancy between the goal he sets for himself and the strength nature granted him when he came into the world.' The feeling of the painful discrepancy in their ability to achieve a goal that they deeply care about is the internal crisis that can provoke people to learn.

JRD Tata often said that Sumant Moolgaokar was a great developer of men. In truth, both of them were, and the way they both did it was to give their protégés gifts—gifts in the form of challenges that made them learn. Having first thrust me into Pune when I felt I was far from ready, some years later Moolgaokar gave me another gift. By then I had found my stride in Pune. We had successfully created a new and innovative human resource management systems to enable Telco to find, motivate, and rapidly develop the thousands of craftsmen, engineers, and managers the company needed. I was completely absorbed and fulfilled by my work. The spirit of the people was palpable, as was noted by VS Naipaul, the Nobel Prize winning author, when he visited the factory. The people were confidently learning and applying new skills to make a factory, which they and their country would be proud of.

A matter of honour

One day, early in 1977, I went to meet Sumant Moolgaokar in Mumbai. I wanted his agreement in principle to the approach we would take in the forthcoming negotiations with the unions. When I arrived, I found he was busy in an emergency meeting with some senior executives and directors of the company. He invited me to listen to the discussions. They were discussing a serious crisis in Tatab Industries in Malaysia, a company that Telco had been invited to join as a technical collaborator and investor by the Tengku Arif Bendahara, whose older brother was soon to be crowned the King of Malaysia.

Malaysia had become independent and free from British rule some 20 years after India. Like India, Malaysia had felt it was exploited by its colonial rulers, having been the supplier of raw materials for feeding the British industry. Like India, it wanted to create its own industries. And like India, it introduced a system of industrial licensing to manage the investments flowing into various sectors. However, there were two significant differences in the policies of the two countries. One was the objective of Malaysian government policy to give the *bumiputras—*

the native Malays—an opportunity to catch up with the local Chinese who, along with British companies and often in partnership with them, had dominated the business sector during the colonial regime. The other was that Malaysia was not yet as interested as India in creating depth in its industry.

In the 1970s, there were already several makes of cars from various countries that were being sold in Malaysia: Mercedes, Peugeot, Toyota, Nissan, Mazda, Volvo, Ford, and many others. There were also many brands of trucks and buses: Mercedes, Ford, Bedford (General Motors), Volvo, Nissan, and Mitsubishi to name a few. When licences were issued, these companies were permitted to continue to sell in the country, provided they arranged to assemble their products locally. Malaysia did not wish to deprive its people of the choice of products, but at the same time wanted in some way to add value and create jobs in the country. It also wanted to bring more *bumiputras* into business. In the already crowded truck and bus industry, the government of the state of Sarawak in Eastern Malaysia was granted a licence to assemble Hino (Toyota) vehicles. Tengku Arif Bendahara, who was a rising *bumiputra* business star, cajoled the government to also give him a license. He needed a partner to set up the plant and he persuaded Telco to join him. Thus Tatab Industries was born as a joint venture between the Tatas and Tengku Arif Bendahara (Tab, for short).

The arrangement between Telco and Tab was modelled on the successful arrangement between Daimler Benz and Telco, with Telco playing the role of the German company and Tengku's company taking up the role the Tatas had in India. But the two situations were not similar, and therein lay the seeds of the problem that led to the crisis. Whereas the Tatas had created and managed businesses successfully in India for over 70 years, when they invited Daimler Benz to join them in a collaboration to produce commercial vehicles in India, Tengku's fledgling company had no previous experience in managing an industrial enterprise. Therefore, an arrangement modelled on the lines of the collaboration between the Indians and Germans could not work out because there was no one at the Malaysian end to play the managerial role which the Tatas had played in India. The Indian technical managers deputed by Telco were counting on the Malaysians to run the board and manage the finances and were blissfully unaware of the brewing storm. By early 1977, the lenders to the company had had enough of the mismanagement of finances and decided to withdraw their loan. This would have plunged the company into bankruptcy. The bankers arrived in India to ask what remedy the Tatas had in mind. The Tata group members were shocked to learn how bad the situation was. A senior team from Telco, led by two directors, was sent to Malaysia to make a first-hand assessment and suggest a solution. This team had just returned and when I walked into the meeting they were reporting to Sumant Moolgaokar, Chairman and CEO, and Nani Palkhiwala, Deputy Chairman of Telco.

Their report was shocking. While the factory was coming up quite well, tucked away amongst the thick jungles of the state of Pahang, supervised by Indian managers, all else was falling apart in the company. Dealers who had been appointed by Tengku's company were suing the company for non-performance of contracts. Customers who had been sold vehicles that Tengku's company had been permitted to import in order to introduce the Tata trucks into the market had not received promised service and parts. Suppliers had not been paid and some were threatening to remove the equipment they had supplied to the new factory. Finances were in disarray. The management team (if it could be called that!) comprising the Indian technical managers and local managers looking after the sales and finances were at loggerheads, blaming each other for the mess. The competition was solidly established. Daimler Benz, Telco's own teacher, was highly respected in Malaysia and had the largest market share. General Motors, the world's largest company, was second. Hino, the commercial vehicle wing of the formidable Toyota, was rapidly climbing to third position. Meanwhile, Tengku and his friends on the board continued to party at his house every week, drinking only Dom Perignon champagne as he proudly boasted and sending the bills to Tatab Industries. Nero fiddling while Rome burns around him? Not quite. Nero was at least aware that Rome was burning. Tengku's cronies were unaware of the problems of the company they managed and ironically they blamed the Indian managers for keeping them in the dark. Everyone was blaming everyone else for the problems! Consequently, no one seemed to be in control.

The bankers were very firm. The only conditions under which they were willing to continue the loan was a change in the top management of the company and a guarantee from the Tatas that the company would begin to make profits in the next three years. However, government regulations prevented the Tatas from providing either of these guarantees. This was the era in which India was starved of foreign exchange. The Indian government did not permit Indian companies from sending money outside the country or entering into any contracts that may require them to do so. Therefore the Tatas could not offer more than a comfort letter, and that too only if they could themselves be assured that the company could be turned around so rapidly. To do this, the team's report to Moolgaokar was clear: The company needed a new CEO to turn it around, a person in whose ability and integrity the Tatas had full faith. Unfortunately, the licence granted by the Malaysian government stipulated that the CEO had to be a *bumiputra*.

Nani Palkhiwala immediately drafted a letter to Tengku Arif asking him to obtain an exception from the Malaysian government to permit a Tata executive to manage Tatab Industries for at least three years. If Tengku got this permission, Palkhiwala wrote, the Tatas would depute a suitable person and consider giving an assurance to the bankers so that the company, and Tengku's reputation, could be saved. In truth, the Tatas were also very concerned about their own international reputation. Palkhiwala was a brilliant lawyer and he attended to the legal problems. All eyes were now on Moolgaokar for an answer to the other problem. Who would the Tatas send as CEO if the Malaysian government gave permission?

Moolgaokar asked the team to describe the knowledge and experience that the CEO must have and which individuals may be likely candidates. Several things needed to be taken care of. The board would have to be restructured. The dealer network had to be reorganised. The customers' confidence was in shambles. The entire process of brand building had to be done. Finances had to be put in order and loans had to be renegotiated. The job seemed daunting. When the discussion stopped, Moolgaokar turned with a smile to me, the man who had dropped in into the meeting, and gave me the gift of the challenge!

The others were nonplussed since I was the least qualified, and the youngest. I thought Moolgaokar was joking. But he confirmed what he said. I would go to Malaysia and do whatever was required to turn around Tatab Industries in three years. He asked me to call my wife and let her know that the family could join me in a few weeks.

Soon I was on a plane to Malaysia. I knew very little about the country. On the plane I browsed through an introduction to Malaysia, and also a little book I was lucky to find in the bookshop at the Taj Mahal hotel in Mumbai. The book was a collection of stories about Malaya before its independence, written by a Frenchman, Henri Fauconnier. The book's title, *The Soul of Malaya*, had intrigued me. A chapter in the book began with the expression, 'Malaya, where there is still time to kill time'. It was the most ironic expression I could have read.

The Malaysian government were persuaded by Tengku Arif to give permission for the Tatas to send a CEO so that Tatab, the only *bumiputra* company in the truck business could be saved. The government wanted to build success stories for its *bumiputra* policy and could not afford big failures. But they gave permission for only two years, and not three. It looked like I would certainly not have any time to kill in Malaysia.

The last piece of advice given to me by Telco's Finance Director, who had led the inquiry team to Malaysia, was to replace the entire executive team of Tatab. Tengku Arif, whom I met when I arrived, gave me the same advice. A man can only be as good as his team, he said, and my team was rotten. They were incompetent and untrustworthy according to him. He felt particularly let down by the Indian executives within the team, whom he had looked after very well. They were earning much more money in Malaysia than they had in India. Tatab was providing them with new Mercedes and Peugeots, whereas in India they would be lucky to have a new car, if they had one at all. (In those days, Indians were hardly permitted to travel abroad, or import foreign goods, and salaries in India were not high.) He said the Indians seemed to be in Malaysia to have a good time and make money.

The executives definitely did not make a team. Relations between them had broken down completely, particularly under pressure from bankers, dealers, and irate customers. When I landed in Kuala Lumpur, I found the Service Manager, an Indian, in hospital. The stress was too much for him. He accused the Sales Manager, a Chinese, of having his wife's dog strangled by Chinese gangsters and left on their doorstep. Both of them accused the Indian Plant Manager of living in a world of his own, oblivious of the demands of dealers. The Administration Manager, a Malay, was convinced that the Sales Manager had his hand in the till. So here I was, totally innocent about Malaysia, with no experience in critical functions such as marketing and sales, and with no one to rely on. If I fired the top executives as I was advised, how would I go about finding their replacements in a country I did not know? And how long would it take? Would the better strategy not be to fire up these same people and make a winning team with them, I wondered?

When I told them that the board had given me a challenge to turn around the company in three years, their first reaction was to point out the difficulty of doing it. The second reaction was to point a finger at the board's culpability for the mess. I did not want to go down those paths. I had to prove a lot in a very short time: The trustworthiness of Tatas as partners; the quality of Telco engineering and products; and my capability as a manager. To achieve these, the company had to turn around. It dawned on me that what really inspired me to take on a seemingly impossible task was the superordinate goal of restoring the reputation of my company and my country. I wondered what the deeper goals and aspirations of the senior executives were.

I confided in my Indian colleagues that I was pained by the sniggering in Malaysia about the ability of Indian managers in comparison with Japanese and European managers. And I mentioned that people were of the opinion that we were in Malaysia primarily to acquire refrigerators, kitchen gadgets, and music systems to take back to India. I told them that I would voluntarily reduce my own salary and return the Mercedes car the board had given me. I was not asking them to do the same. I merely wanted them to know what I was up to.

The board was surprised. Tengku argued with me that my salary was very reasonable for a CEO in Malaysia and the car was necessary to maintain the dignity of the company. But I was firm. I would much rather have him arguing that I had too little than that I had too much. With a clear conscience, I also returned Tengku's bills for the Dom Perignon champagne served at his parties.

The team rallied around quickly. First the Indians spoke to me about their desire to prove their worth as managers, and their deep aspiration to make a mark for India. They all reduced their own salaries. They bonded with each other through their shared commitment to a higher purpose. Their commitment to a higher cause also earned them new respect from their Chinese and Malay colleagues. In turn the local managers came to me and shared their aspirations to prove themselves in Malaysia amongst their professional peers and the business community. All of us recognised that we had similar, deep, personal aspirations and that the only way we could realise them was by working together to take on what seemed to be an impossible task. There were no more arguments with the board and no more accusations about each other. We were just going to do it.

What that team achieved and what each of the executives accomplished became a legend in the industry. The net result was that vehicles proudly wearing the Tata badge rapidly overtook the competition. They outsold all other brands in the country within two years, at prices higher than Japanese vehicles. Prices had to be kept high to achieve the target of making profits in three years. In fact the company made profits within two years. The bankers and the board were delighted.

My two years were up. It was time to come home to Pune. The Tatas had beaten Mercedes Benz, and also Hino, Toyota's commercial vehicle arm. Hino had been revving up to overtake the other European brands when the Tatas arrived. But the Tatas had come from behind and overtaken them. The CEO of Hino graciously invited me to a farewell meeting in his office. I was accompanied by one of my Indian colleagues. The Japanese CEO had five of his countrymen with him. Over tea he said that the Tatas' performance was remarkable. He commented how immature the local Malaysian managers were. He was sure that we had lots of expatriate managers from India.

He inquired how many there were. I said, 'Five.' 'No, not in your office, Mairasan, in the whole company?' he asked. I repeated my answer. He paused in awe, and then stood up and bowed, his Japanese colleagues with him. 'We are 20 Japanese altogether in my company. You five Indians have beaten us. Mairasan, one Indian equals five Japanese!' he said.

The recognition that Indians were not less than managers from any other part of the globe was the aspirational goal we had set out to achieve. This goal gave us the emotional energy to overcome all technical and managerial challenges on the way. I had not yet come across Peter Senge's work and Robert Fritz's research of the concept of creative tension. (Nor had I read Alexander the Great's biography.) Therefore I did not yet have the words to express the profound lesson I had learned about the power of a shared aspirational vision to glue a team and stretch it to achieve the seemingly impossible. As it happened, I got yet another chance to affirm this lesson in practice in Pune before I found the research to explain it in the USA.

Better than the best

I returned to the factory in Pune that had grown in the two years I was away. Telco, with its two factories in Jamshedpur and Pune, dominated the Indian commercial vehicle industry with 70 per cent of the market for medium and heavy trucks. Indian manufacturers of light commercial vehicles were relatively very weak. Therefore, the demand for lighter commercial vehicles was mostly met by second-hand Tata vehicles. They were strong and durable and having served for heavy duty applications for a few years, comfortably did lighter duty for many more. Thereby the resale prices for Tata vehicles were high and overall demand for Tata vehicles had received a boost.

This happy state of affairs for Telco was threatened by the arrival of Japanese truck manufacturers in India. Toyota, Nissan, Mitsubishi, and Mazda were permitted by the Indian government to sell vehicles to fill the need for new light commercial vehicles in India. This would hit the resale of second-hand Tata vehicles, which in turn would hurt the sale of new vehicles. More ominously, once the Japanese established their quality and built their dealer networks in India, they could, as a next step, move up into direct competition with Telco in the medium truck market. Telco had to stop the Japanese before they became too strong in India. But Telco's hands were tied by government rules. The company was not permitted to produce vehicles lighter than 6 tonnes gross weight.

The company pleaded with the government. It had worked hard to build capabilities in Pune to design new models of vehicles and design the machines and dies required to manufacture them. If the Japanese could be permitted to fill the need for light vehicles in India, why not Telco? The bureaucrats argued that the foreign exchange quota for the light vehicle industry had been exhausted with allotments to the Japanese for the import of CKD (completely knocked down) packs and for payments of royalties by their Indian partners. Therefore, they said, Telco could have the government's permission provided it did not import any technology, parts, or machines to make light vehicles. Telco had no option but to take on the challenge.

A lot of time had been lost in the haggling! Meanwhile the Japanese had advanced into the market, signing up dealers and selling vehicles. The only way to make a serious dent in their advance now was to surprise them by designing, engineering, and producing a new vehicle in about 18 months. Back then, the best time in the world to develop a new truck model was about four years. Telco would have to create a world record in product development to beat the Japanese. Could Telco, an *Indian* company, do this?

I could sense the mood change in the room when this question was posed at a meeting of managers in Pune. The heads of the many divisions in Pune were meeting to consider what they would do, since the government had given them the go ahead. With that question, I could see a glint come into many eyes. Some people leaned back and crossed their hands behind their heads. Others leaned forward, hands on knees. And some began to smile. I could feel them saying to themselves, 'Now wouldn't *that* be something!' 'But how?' was the next question on everybody's minds. It appeared the government had really tied our hands with the restrictions imposed. We would have to do everything ourselves. 'Maybe that is why we can do it faster than anyone else has done it before,' someone suggested. 'Where else in the world would you have all the disciplines required to design a truck, the production team, and all the people who will design and make the machines and the tools required to manufacture the truck, in the same room every day as we have in Pune?' he asked.

All over the world, studies have shown that confusion and delays in new product development take place at the handovers between the many disciplines involved. These are popularly known as 'over the wall' interactions. The design division throws the product blueprints over the wall to the manufacturing division. The manufacturing division examines them, finds several faults and throws them back to design for corrections. When the designs are acceptable, the manufacturing division begins the same 'over the wall' process with suppliers of machines and dies. With them, the walls are even higher because they are separate companies and prices have to be negotiated and contracts established. 'What if we were to work like one integrated team without any walls between us? Could we not reduce the time for product development very considerably?' someone else asked. Thus Project Jupiter was born with the goals to produce a light truck in 18 months with an innovative team-based approach, which eventually beat the Japanese in India.

Very soon, someone stood up and said, 'Let us work backwards. If the completed product has to be in the dealers' showrooms along with spare parts and service manuals in eighteen months, what is the immediate preceding milestone that must be achieved?' The next question was what would be required to come in the step before that. Thus, working backwards, with tighter and tighter times for every step, an overall plan was sketched out with the first step being the production of a working prototype in only one month (whereas it usually took several months)! The prototype is traditionally the responsibility of the design and product development division in any company. But every division in Pune chipped in with resources of people and machines to help the product development division. The next month saw people work together like they had never before, and the prototype was ready on time. The team continued with the inspired spirit of cooperation, finding innovative solutions through the steps that followed the prototype. The vehicle was introduced in 18 months. It was Telco's great success. It built the foundation for Telco's continuing inroads into lighter vehicles and thus Telco was able to dislodge the Japanese before they could establish themselves.

The lesson is, when people connect with what they deeply care about, and realise they cannot obtain it unless they go beyond prevalent ideas to new ones, they generate a 'creative tension' in themselves. This condition of 'creative tension' stimulates the discovery of new solutions. The aspiration to be recognised as the best managers in the world, and not the profits that Tatab would make, inspired the team in Malaysia to achieve what seemed impossible. Similarly, it was the aspiration of creating a world record and thereby beating the Japanese, and not the sales and profits Telco would make from a light truck, that inspired the team of Project Jupiter.

A shared vision, not a vision shared

I learned much later from my colleague in Innovation Associates, Dr Brian Smith, the conceptual difference between a 'vision shared' and a 'shared vision'. This helped me understand the power of a vision when it is directly connected with people's personal aspirations. CEOs with a vision are admired across the world. They are expected to communicate their vision to motivate the troops. Often, they do so through their vision statements. In this way, a vision—that of the CEO—is shared with the organisation.

This is a 'vision shared'. The other approach is to ask people what they care about deeply and to initiate a process of change that builds on their aspirations as well and not merely on those of the CEO. A theoretical objection to the latter process is often the concern that the aspirations of the people may not align with those of the CEO. To this, the answer is that it is always wise for a commander-in-chief to know the state of mind of his or her troops and not presume that they are as committed to his/her objectives as he/she may be. Fortunately, very often, the aspirations of the people and their leaders are aligned, even if they do not know about it. So to discover that they can all achieve their aspirations, provided they work together to achieve an overarching goal, creates a tremendous force for change and achievement.

I saw yet again the power of a 'shared vision', similar to the one I had experienced in Malaysia and Pune. This time it was in Mexico City. The mayor of the city, which is one of the largest in the world with a population exceeding 10 million, asked Arthur D Little Inc (ADL), the American company I was consulting with at that time, for help. An election was coming up in a few months and the mayor wanted to improve the civil services in order to win votes. The problem was that the municipal workers, numbering about 100,000, were uneducated, lazy, and uncooperative, according to the mayor (and the citizens of Mexico City also, for that matter!). He had shared with them his vision of a clean and efficient city. He had exhorted them through slogans and meetings to cooperate with him towards improving municipal services.

The team from ADL organised a vision workshop with the workers of one of the precincts of the city. They asked the workers what mattered most to them. The answer, after some reflection, was: Respect. But respect from whom, they were asked. Their neighbours, they said. Municipal workers were reputed to be lazy, uneducated and inefficient, and so their neighbours did not really respect them. Moreover, their children did not like to admit or disclose their fathers' occupation to their friends in school. Thus the deepest aspiration of the municipal workers was to obtain respect from society, whereas their union leaders and managers, including the mayor, thought that what the workers wanted most of all was more money!

The workers were asked to consider what would make then neighbours respect them. After some debate amongst themselves, they volunteered that respect would come to them if citizens saw municipal services improve in a remarkable way. The next question was, what they could do to improve the services and thereby get what they deeply aspired for. The drift of what happened in the next few months, would by now be apparent to the reader. The mayor and the citizens were amazed at the change in attitude, behaviour, and service provided by the workers of that precinct. However the so-called softer, aspirational approach to change was not followed in other precincts. In those places the more traditional, directive, and harder approach was adopted. The overall improvement in the city was spotty, and the mayor unfortunately lost the election. Nevertheless, the power of one approach over the other had been confirmed.

Everyone in an organisation, down to the lowest level of employee, is a valuable resource and should be involved in developing the vision of the organisation. This is an idea that two Indian CEOs took to instinctively. They wanted everyone in their organisation to be involved in creating the vision. One of them was U Sundarajan of BPCL, who was the first to involve all of the 2000-strong management staff along with other staff comprising 8000 people of his company in the process of vision creation. He was determined to make BPCL a faster learning organisation, and he did succeed. The company's success in developing new services has been greatly admired in the country. It is one of India's most successful corporate transformation stories.

The other CEO was B Muthuraman of Tata Steel. In the ninetees, the turnaround of Tata Steel by Muthuraman's predecessor, Jamshed Irani, to make the company the lowest cost steel producer in the world is well known. When I returned to India this success story was one of the most frequently cited examples at management conventions in 2000. Muthuraman succeeded Irani as CEO in 2002. The company could easily rest on its laurels. Muthuraman wanted the people, all 40,000 of them, to spur themselves to even greater achievements. I explained to him the difference in the power between a 'vision shared' and a 'shared vision'. His instincts said that the company needed a 'shared vision'. He set aside the vision statement he was drafting and determined to invite all 40,000 employees to shape the vision. His managers also liked the concept of a 'shared vision', but did not know how they could develop one in just three months, a deadline Muthuraman had already declared to announce the new vision of the company. Surely, they said, there would be circumstances such as a crisis in which it is appropriate, and indeed necessary, for the CEO to announce his vision. Perhaps one should not be carried away too far with the idea of a 'shared vision' of all employees, they suggested.

But Muthuraman had seen a vision. There was a gleam in his eye. The gleam from a vision of all 40,000 employees having the opportunity to contribute to the company's vision. He was not to be stopped. Over the next three months, all 40,000 employees were given an opportunity to articulate their vision. The company galvanised its structure of participatory forums that it had built over many decades. It supplemented this structure with new, Internet-based communications technology. Thus workmen in remote mines and collieries could also make their contributions. In three months, Muthuraman was able to announce the shared vision for Tata Steel that its people had developed.

An aspirational vision—like the gleam in the eye of Muthuraman, or the dream in the heart of Alexander, or the inner yearning of the Mexican municipal worker—has the power to stretch the imagination and open the mind to new ideas. However, while vision—the 'Know Want' (in the Learning Field—is necessary to create conditions for learning and change, it is not enough for solving intractable problems. Einstein said that we cannot solve difficult problems with the same way of thinking that brought us into those problems. The next chapter turns from aspirations to our ways of thinking. The deeply imbedded theories and 'Know Whys' that exist inside our heads.

Looking for a Crisis of Aspiration

The people who will be the beneficiaries of the development process should determine the goals of development and the type of society they want; the goals cannot be determined by economists

'Do we need another crisis to get India together to take some tough decisions to improve our economy?' mused one of India's leading economists in April 2002. He was a key member of the team that had heralded in economic reforms in the early 1990s when India had been on the brink of default. 'We are drifting again', he said. 'Not too bad and not too good. Meanwhile the problem of unemployment is growing. But it is very difficult to get people to agree to the decisions that must be taken.' I also heard business managers say that it is more difficult to mobilise people when there is no evident crisis. But it should not have to be this way. Crisis and fear are undoubtedly very effective catalysts to collective action, and good leaders know how to take advantage of them when they

Article first published in *The Economic Times.*

arise. However, the problem with using crisis or fear as a motivator is that the need to keep moving is diminished when the crisis passes. This then confronts the leaders with the question of whether one must wait for another crisis to happen, or evoke a crisis to bring people together again!

A better way to get people moving is to create an attraction— an aspirational vision that draws people towards the same goal. The economist agreed. 'We clearly have a problem of communication in India: people must see what is in it for them.' There is a world of meaning in the simple expression 'see what is in it for them'. To see means to visualise. And 'what is in it for them' means people who are expected to take a journey together should be able to visualise in their minds what the outcome of the journey will eventually feel like to them. However, most communications by economists and others who want to provide direction to countries express the outcomes of development as numbers about the performance of the economy. People cannot visualise what the numbers would mean as images of real things around them. What they want to know is, 'What would my life be like if this change is brought about?'

The last 50 years have seen a massive release of human aspiration in the world as colonialism receded and over a hundred sovereign nations joined the international pantheon, each seeking to stand proud. All of them knew that they had to be economically strong if they were to matter. Thus began their search for the means of effective economic development. And many turned to economists to guide them, whence began the growth of the profession of developmental economics, with increasing numbers of economists in international developmental institutions and national planning commissions. However, the focus of the emerging profession was almost entirely on the means for economic development, as HW Arndt points out in his book, *Economic Development: The History of an Idea.* The dialogue about the goals of development, and how development should change the nature of societies and the lives and cultures of people was generally outside the ambit of the discussions of the new economic scientists. Thus the dialogue amongst the people for whom development is required was left to politicians and NGOs, and when their suggestions would not fit the equations of economists and businessmen, they came to be seen as troublesome and ill-informed meddlers in the systematic growth of economies.

In at least one fundamental way the development of the capability of societies is not unlike the process of transformation of corporations that, in a competitive world, have to continuously improve capabilities and performance. People have to be engaged with the process of change and must be able to visualise the potential outcomes in terms that mean something to them personally. In a Mexican company that set itself on a path to international growth and radical performance improvement, the outcome of successful change was visualised by the CEO as that moment when his picture would be on the cover of *Business Week*. The maintenance worker in the factory visualised a happy place to work in and a place of pride in his local community. Both would get what they aspired to if the transformation was successful. Moreover, the worker was able to visualise how the steps of change would lead to the outcome he aspired to, just as the CEO could see the possibility for himself. Everyone admitted that their current reality with which they were comfortable was far short of what they aspired to. This painful discrepancy created a crisis of aspiration. This helped to align people, and there was a great commitment through the process of transformation. The desired outcomes were obtained: the CEO was on the cover of *Business Week*, and the company became a global benchmark for operational excellence through participatory practices. The lesson throughout history has been that great leaders of societies and companies enable people to visualise the aspirational goals they all desire to achieve and thereby often commit to painful change. It is time that we paint together, through dialogue, a meaningful picture of the India we want. Or else we will slip from *chalta hai* to a crisis situation.

President Abdul Kalam has propounded a vision for transforming India into a 'developed country' by 2020. However, there are two questions that arise in this regard. First, what does this vision mean to the people at large? And second, how will this vision make change actually happen? The President's vision was presented to a conclave in Kochi on the occasion of Máta Amritandamayi's 50th birthday in 2003. The conclave included businessmen from India and the US, scientists, educationists, doctors, social workers, and others. An Indian scientist who had been involved with its preparation presented the vision. When he finished, someone said that the vision, though good, described a scientist's view of what India should be and that other perspectives should be added for a more complete vision for the development of the country.

Speaking at the same conclave, Professor CK Prahalad presented his vision of an India whose gross domestic product (GDP) grows at 10 per cent per annum. To the first six facets of this vision, which he had presented before at CII, he added a seventh this time. This was a vision of a country built upon its diversity. He said that only by harnessing its diversity could India hope to realise the other six economic facets of its vision.

India set out in 1947 with a vision of being a secular country that would celebrate its diversity. But in the past two years the vision of secularism has become very muddied. The controversy in the country about Mark Tully's documentary for BBC shows that we are not even in agreement about what we mean by secularism. To some, secularism connotes an absence of religiosity. To others it means a plurality of religions thriving together. What do we want our country to be? A country with one religion? Many religions? Or do we not want to be identified with any religion at all? Surely an agreement about this must be the cornerstone of any meaningful vision for India.

At the Kochi conclave, a very successful Indian entrepreneur from Silicon Valley described his vision for India to the President. Along with reduction in poverty, universal education, and faster growth in GDP, this entrepreneur added that India must become a proper capitalist country. The President agreed that we must remove poverty and become developed. But above all, he said, we want happiness for our people. Therefore, he said that we should not get stuck with words such as capitalist and socialist. In fact, if necessary we should find another non-controversial word that explains what we really want.

Why should we waste time debating about the meanings of words, you may ask? Why don't we 'Just Do It', as the famous Nike slogan has suggested. This was the same advice that the Silicon Valley entrepreneur repeated at Kochi. (Though we should be sceptical at this time about simplistic advice from California about how to manage an economy!) The question is what is 'it'? If we want the money and time of our non-resident Indian (NRI) entrepreneur to be part of 'it', he must want 'it'. And if we want the people in the streets and farms of India to cooperate with 'it', and do their bit to make it happen, they too should want 'it'. The power of a shared vision, for countries and organisations, lies in the commitment it can create to work towards the desired goals. Without that heart-felt commitment, the vision is reduced to mere decoration in glossy brochures and on office walls. People cannot commit to something that they do not really understand or want. Therein lies the value, nay necessity, of participation of diverse people in shaping the vision of a 'developed' India.

But will it not take a long time to get many people involved? And, is it feasible to get an alignment of views amongst people with different perspectives? I would respond by asking how much time each of us spends at meetings merely listening to the same things being said by the same people. Add up all that time. Could some of this time not be allocated to another type of dialogue between diverse people that may lead to fresh insights and commitments towards shared goals? I would also suggest that people are more willing to hear others if they feel they are being heard as well. Dialogue is a two-way process. Unfortunately, most of our meetings are monologues by a few and not dialogues amongst many. They are replete with power-point presentations and rambling speeches. The output of such meetings is very small compared to the time put in by all the participants.

Finally, if we agree that India must learn how to combine its diversity into a powerhouse, and if we also know that a shared vision of development is required, then by all means let us 'Just Do It'! The 'it' is to quickly and effectively engage many people, representing the different facets of India, in determining the quality of the country we wish to have and will work together in order to create. To those who would say that such a participative process is necessary but not feasible, I would say that if we all desire an India that is innovative (as all of the vision presenters in Kochi, including the President, had emphasised), let us immediately apply our innovative abilities to devise a process that will work positively.

Without Shared Visions Empires will Collapse

A shared vision may be a better means to keep people working together than the sway of charismatic leadership or the greed for rewards and fear of punishments

ABOUT 2400 years ago, Alexander the Great created a vast empire of territories stretching from Macedonia to India. Within a few years of his death, the empire had collapsed. In the last century, the Soviet Union grew into a mighty force and suddenly imploded. In the world of business, Harold Geneen rapidly created a vast international conglomerate of companies called ITT, ranging from mining to telecommunications to hotels. He was a business legend in his lifetime but could not save his empire from collapsing. Nor could the powerful Kenneth Lay prevent Enron, the much-hyped group of new-age businesses, from evaporating suddenly. All these conglomerations of countries and businesses seemed to lack the glue to hold them together once the fission within them began.

Article first published in *The Economic Times*.

Many business gurus say that the forces that have been unleashed by globalisation will make the diversified conglomerate as extinct as the dodo. They say it is imperative for companies to be focussed if they want to survive. On the other hand, some experts cite General Electric (GE) and other successful conglomerates to suggest that there is something that the leaders of such conglomerates do which results in the value of the whole becoming even greater than the sum of the parts.

What is the value to the part of belonging to the whole? What is the value that the centre provides to these diverse parts? What is the nature of the glue that holds disparate nations and businesses together? What is the role of leaders in organisations that are composed of diverse parts? These should be amongst the most important questions on the minds of political and business leaders as nations come together and as businesses connect across global boundaries. Certainly these are important questions for Indian political leaders as power devolves to states and for leaders of Indian business conglomerates as they shape up.

Let us look into the four examples of organisations that fell apart. Alexander set out to pursue a vision of personal greatness. From accounts of his life, such as *Alexander: The Ends of the Earth* by Valerio Manfredi, it is evident that his soldiers were loyal to him personally, rather than inspired by his dream of an empire. Their bond broke with his death, and there was nothing more to hold the empire together. Harold Geneen was notorious for his business review meetings in which he publicly embarrassed his executives. They were driven by fear of the boss. The Soviet Union collapsed once the power of the communist idea that had united people in the Soviet Union died in their hearts and the leaders also lost the will to impose their authority by fear. In Enron, the motivating force driving executives in the company was personal wealth. It was an example, perhaps in the extreme, of what happens if personal gain begins to matter most to the members of an organisation.

These examples suggest that in order to hold a nation or an

organisation together, prevalent theories-in-use of how people are held together may be inappropriate. First, reliance on charismatic leadership is not a sustainable strategy. Second, organisations built on economic incentives and fear of punishment as the principal means for motivating people are fragile. I deliberately use the expression theory-in-use to distinguish it from an espoused theory. An espoused theory is what we may say we believe in. The theory-in-use is what we actually do. For example, we are always looking for that single leader to whom we can attribute the success of a nation or an organisation. The media also loves stories of larger-than-life heroes. Hence our theory-in-use is the belief in charismatic leaders at the top, even if our espoused theory is distributed leadership. Similarly, whereas we may espouse the view that people do not work only for money, the belief in the power of the market and economic incentives has been the principal theory-in-use in the design of reward systems in the last decade.

I would suggest that the theory we must act on is that the glue that cements organisations of diverse peoples and businesses, and the driving motivation for their members has to be a shared and deeply held vision of what the whole can be. Therefore the first role of leaders at the centre is to create this shared vision. I must distinguish here between a 'vision shared' and a 'shared vision'. Vision statements crafted by the centre and told to the rest of the organisation are a 'vision shared'. They do not have the magnetic power to hold organisations together and to motivate people that visions that are alive in the minds and hearts of people have. The second role of leaders is to create platforms for the diverse parts to work with each other and learn together as they shape the whole in ways that fulfil the aspirations of the individual parts as well. The processes for these dialogues in which shared visions come to life, and learning moves across boundaries, are required to keep our nations and conglomerates together in healthy wholes. Therein may lie the answers to the questions we had earlier asked in this piece.

5

Changing

Our

Clocks

Look, we are really fortunate—the Sensex must have gone up still further!

5

Changing Our Clocks

Then he asked for the time of day:
I looked into his eyes and saw God
Had given him seasons and aeons
While I had just my watch
To guide me on my way

—Arun Maira, 'The Old Man on the Mountain'

I had not met anyone before the Indian elections in 2004 who thought that the Congress party would get more votes than the BJP. Nor had I read any analysis, or heard anything on TV that suggested the BJP would lose and they did. As soon as the election results came in, the analysts began to say and all those people I had spoken to began to agree that masses of people out there were not happy with the progress in the economy. Obviously, the indicators that 'people like us' had been paying attention to could not tell us what was really going on in the country. Two principal indicators of the health of the economy for business people seem to be the stock market index and the views of foreign rating agencies. The information from both these gauges said that India's economy was doing fine at last. Though perhaps it was not. Nevertheless, many people continued to watch the same indicators even after the elections, to gauge which way the economy was headed.

Many of us have become addicted to watching the stock market index. We observe its gyrations anxiously. We feel good when it is going up momentarily and worry when it starts going down. We use it to confirm the efficacy of decisions even as they are being made, although their effect on the economy will take some time and would be modulated by many other factors. I was watching one of our national business news channels on the morning that the new Prime Minister was announcing his plans. One reporter in Delhi was following his speech, while another stood outside the stock exchange in Mumbai checking the reactions of the market. In one corner of the screen was that most important gauge, the stock market index, dancing up and down like an electro-cardiac graph above a patient in an ICU. The Prime Minister said he would moderate the disinvestment programme for public sector units (PSUs). Immediately the reporter in Mumbai said that the market had reacted badly to the news, because the index fell a few points. (It came up again, perhaps reassured by an announcement on another subject.) Later in the programme, the anchor in Delhi repeated that the market had not liked the disinvestment policy because the former had spiked when he spoke about it. The anchor implied therefore that the policy would not be good for the country. I wondered, however, whether the more serious problem for the country than that of the PSU issue could be the PLU (people like us) syndrome. Perhaps we are out of touch and do not know what is really going on in the country.

A concept (model, or 'theory-in-use' as Chris Argyris calls it) in our heads focusses our attention on information that is consistent with our internal model. We ignore other information because it seems irrelevant to us. The information we continue to rely on, consistent with our model, reinforces the model further. I wondered how one could unlearn a concept that may have worked well so far, to make room for a new and even better one? This question had preoccupied my mind when I went into consulting in the USA. My job, very often, was to help clients change the way they approached a problem. I would diligently gather evidence to make my point. However, very often a client would say that the information seemed irrelevant. Some would politely say that maybe Indians and Americans thought differently. The problem it seemed to me was not that we were from different nationalities but that we had different models in our heads. It was dawning on me that consulting at its best has to be the art of helping people achieve what they really want to achieve by holding a mirror to them in which they can see what they otherwise cannot see, viz. the theories at the back of their heads.

One morning as I drove back from a visit to a client's factory in Indiana, USA, I had an unusual encounter with a farmer. I had stopped to buy fruit at a roadside farm stand. We did not haggle about the price of the fruit as we may have done in India, but we haggled about the time of day! The farmer and I could not agree on what the time was. 'It's eleven o'clock,' I said, looking at my watch. 'Not here. Here it is ten o'clock,' said he. 'But it was close to eleven o'clock when I stopped at the gas station a couple of miles back. In fact the attendant confirmed it,' I protested. 'Ah, but that was across the county line, you see,' he explained. 'It is eleven back where you were and it will be eleven a few miles further on. But here, in our county, it is ten o'clock. Because we do not change to daylight saving time along with the rest of the state and the country. We are good farmers. Our animals like to be fed at the same time every day. They wouldn't understand why one day we came by at dawn and the next day it was an hour after dawn. There's no use showing them the time on my watch!'

I drove on to Indianapolis to catch my flight to Boston, pondering over that unusual encounter. Being sure it is the same time every day regardless of what the clock may say was what his animals and he wanted. As I mused, I recalled a story from a children's book. The town cousin was visiting his country cousin. In the morning the town cousin searched for the weather report on TV to check out the local weather, while the country cousin stuck his head out of the window to find out. In my mind the story turned into the two cousins waking up and wondering what time it was. One looked at his watch and said, 'Seven.' The other looked out of the window and said, 'Early morning—sunrise actually.' I wondered which one had a better grasp of what the real time was?

A few months later I flew with my friends, Charlie and Caroline from Boston, for a three-day meeting with some German friends in Wiesbaden. I set my watch forward by six hours when I arrived in Wiesbaden so that I was synchronised with my hosts and ready to 'do in Rome as the Romans do'. However, Charlie and Caroline decided they would stay in their home time for the three days we were away to reduce the effects of jetlag. Each of us had set our watches to give us the information we wanted to pay attention to. While I connected with Germany, they stayed in Boston. They did not reset their watches so that they could know what time it was in Boston and eat accordingly. When our hosts and I looked at our watches we were synchronised with each other. Therefore I enjoyed wining and dining with our German friends while Charlie and Caroline did their own thing. Unfortunately none of us was able to easily reset our internal body clocks to the new conditions and so all three of us suffered from jetlag when we returned. Though, with the wining and dining, I probably suffered more than they did!

Tallying clocks: Cross-model conversations

The setting of our clocks conditions our behaviour as Charlie, Caroline and I learned with some amusement on our brief visit to Wiesbaden. Many 'clocks' govern our lives. A large number of these are instruments and gauges that we design ourselves to measure phenomena objectively and to enable us to communicate consistently with each other. The watches on our wrists and clocks in our computers serve these purposes. And so do the conventions and indicators of the condition of the business and the economy used by business accountants and economists. However, the models in our heads of what is important to know condition what we choose to observe and measure. If we are not in agreement about what that may be, the precision of the measures we use will not help in improving communication amongst us.

This became evident in a discussion that Lester Thurow, the world renowned economist from the Massachusetts Institute of Technology (MIT) had with a group of economists and business leaders in New Delhi on the benefits of globalisation. Thurow ranked countries by their wealth, beginning with the USA and ending with the countries of Central Africa. As he read the names, he discounted some oil-producing countries with a high GDP per capita because they were 'rich but not developed'. At the end of his talk he pointedly compared India with China in terms of GDP per capita. India fared poorly whether GDP was measured in currency exchange terms or purchasing power parity (PPP). Someone reminded him about his earlier remarks about the oil producing countries. 'You appear to value something other than wealth, called development, Dr Thurow,' he said. 'Yet in judging countries, you use only the monetary measure of GDP. What is the measure of "development"?' 'What about the ability to be happy with less? Is that a measure of development?' another asked. The thought that came to my mind was, 'Is the gauge that Thurow is using telling us what we really want to know?'

Thurow acknowledges in the prologue to his recent book, *Fortune Favors the Bold: What We Must Do to Build a New and Lasting Global Prosperity*, that 'In separating the babble from the facts it is important to understand that the economic tower of Babel looks different depending upon where you stand. It is not that one of these perspectives is right and the others are wrong. Each focuses on different elements of the same tower. All reflect some aspects of the truth.' Our belief about what is important is partially determined by our academic disciplines. For example, anthropologists and economists pay attention to different facets of society. Anthropologists see the heterogeneity of peoples. Economists see the processes of trade and production. What we pay attention to is also influenced by our social, cultural, and political conditioning. Richard Nesbitt points out in *The Geography of Thought: How Asians and Westerners Think Differently and Why*: that 'East Asians attend more to context than Americans do. And what captures one's attention is what one is likely to regard as causally important. The converse seems equally plausible: If one thinks something is causally important one is likely to attend to it. So a cycle gets established whereby theories about causality and focus of attention reinforce each other.'

When we use different gauges to assess the same phenomena it is not surprising that we seem to be talking about different things even if we speak the same language with the same words and grammar. For example, 'Family Values' is a very important theme in the US political debate. Both conservatives and liberals often use the same metaphor of 'family'. However they have different mental models of how a good family functions as George Lakoff points out in *Moral Politics: What Conservatives Know That Liberals Don't*. Conservatism is based on a 'Strict Father' model while liberalism is centred on a 'Nurturant

Parent' model. This, Lakoff says, 'seems to explain why liberals and conservatives seem to be talking about the same thing and yet each reach opposite conclusions—and why they seem to be talking past each other even with little understanding much of the time'.

I cite three experts from three different fields—Thurow, an economist, Nesbitt, a social psychologist, and Lakoff, a cognitive scientist—to highlight something they all point to, namely the difficulty in obtaining an agreement between people with different mental models and different perceptions of what is important to know. David Kantor, a family therapist in Massachusetts, has worked with many families to resolve disputes and rebuild relationships. The most difficult conversations to facilitate are what he calls 'cross-model' conversations. We each have, in our heads, an underlying model of the thing that we are talking about or the metaphor we are using. And when people use the same word or metaphor but attach different meanings, their misunderstandings increase. David's skill lies in helping people understand the models in their own heads as well as in those of others without being judgemental about which is better or worse, and thereby understand each other.

Are we living in the same world?

Consider the terms, globalisation, development, and capitalism. These represent three major forces that are shaping the world. However, as Thurow and many others have pointed out, we do not have a shared view of what we mean by globalisation. And if we do not agree on *what* it is, how can we agree on *how much* it is. No wonder many economists say that the world is no more globalised at the end of the twentieth century than it was at the end of the nineteenth, whereas others say that with the huge onrush of globalisation we are entering a condition that we have never experienced before! Similarly, we do not have an agreement on what we mean by development. Does it merely mean more wealth of the type that can be counted and compared? Or, as the Nobel Prize winning economist Amartya Sen argues, does development include other essential qualities such as 'freedom' that are much harder to measure? And as for capitalism, according to Harold Minsky the economist, there are as many types of capitalism as there are varieties of Heinz pickles. No wonder some capitalists describe others, who see themselves as capitalists, to be socialists!

Whether we like it or not, the whole world is sailing together into the new millennium in a boat which has globalisation and development painted on its prow. And with the demise of communism as a credible system for economic development, capitalism is also being painted alongside. But do we have an agreement about where we may be heading in this boat? To find out, the Aspen Institute organised a seminar on the 'Challenges of Global Capitalism' in August 2002. The participants of the seminar came principally from the USA and India, with a few Europeans as well. Michael Sandel, of the Kennedy School of Government, and author of *Democracy's Discontents*, facilitated an insightful cross-model conversation.

The USA and India are the two largest democracies in the world. Both are capitalist countries. One is highly developed and the other is yet developing. However, geographically they are as far away from each other as two countries can be. India is exactly the other side of the world from the USA. Hence the time difference between the middle of the USA and India is twelve hours. As I participated in the seminar at Aspen, I was reminded of my encounter with the farmer in Indiana. The American farmer and I had been comparing the times on the watches on our wrists, whereas at Aspen, hoping to reveal what really mattered to them, the Americans and Indians would be comparing the time, metaphorically speaking, according to the clocks in their heads. Would we be able to align our clocks, I wondered? Or would we, like Charlie, Caroline, and the Germans in Wiesbaden, continue to live in our separate worlds although we were in the same room?

Can the business of business be only business?

The seminar began with some stories of challenges that business leaders in India and the USA were facing with the advent of globalisation. The Indian story was that of the Tata Steel Company. The Tata Group is a remarkable business organisation. Jamsetji Tata founded it in India over a 100 years back, in the heyday of British colonial rule. He had a vision to make India self-reliant and independent by building industries and scientific institutions. He hired American consulting engineers to help him build a steel plant to exploit the rich iron ore and coal in eastern India barely a 100 miles west of the then British India capital in Calcutta. He envisioned an industrial town that would be green and clean, and which provided for the welfare of the indigenous people (*adivasis*) who lived in the forested hills within which the enterprise would be situated. Jamshedpur, the steel town that was named after him, became a model town, not only for India but also for the model industrial towns of the world. Tata Steel may never have been created if the people of India had not supported it. The British government did not want Indians to have their own industries and tried to derail Jamsetji's scheme. When Jamsetji arrived in London to raise money to build his steel plant, he got a very cold reception. Returning to India disappointed, he was overwhelmed by the offerings of their life savings and jewellery that people brought to his door to invest in his venture.

Over the next 100 years Jamsetji's sons and their successors pioneered many other industries in India from basic chemicals, to trucks, airlines, and computer services. In fact, the first and the largest computer service company in India is the Tata Consultancy Services. It brought Indian software development skills to the USA and other international markets. The principles by which the Tata Group has sought to work since its inception a century ago have been described in *The Creation of Wealth*, an excellent documentation of the history of Tatas by Russi Lala. He describes how the Tatas pursued the creation of not merely personal wealth, but wealth for society. That broad society included the many small shareholders without whose faith the Tata Steel Company could not have completed the steelworks in Jamshedpur. It also included the local communities in which the company operated, the customers for whom the Tatas created products in India that they could not have obtained otherwise, and the country, to which the Tatas have contributed many institutions of research and higher education.

In the early 1990s, India opened its markets and Indian companies began to modernise hastily in order to compete internationally. Tata Steel tightened its belt and embarked on a large investment programme to produce new grades of steel. The company turned to the financial markets for money. When Western-trained financial analysts looked at the company's philosophy of responsibility to society, they were not impressed. They wanted the company to shed its socialist ways and focus itself on shareholder returns. Indian news channels carried hourly reports on the stock markets. Colourful graphs showed the fluctuations in stock prices. The pressure to conform to the requirements of the analysts was high. The managers of the company were in a bind. They wanted to be even better at serving society in many ways and yet look really good to the financial markets. But the measures the market was using placed no value on their contribution to society. The question to the Aspen participants was: 'What advice would you give to the CEO of Tata Steel?'

The first responses from the CEOs gathered at Aspen were predictable. 'The CEO's job is to manage the company to produce wealth for the shareholders.' 'Welcome to the real capitalist world, Tatas!' Over the next few days the participants discussed many other issues associated with globalisation and development—such as the creation of jobs in developing countries, the loss of jobs in some industries in the developed countries, the role and responsibilities of governments, and the role of the media. From these discussions, many fundamental questions followed about the role of business leaders. These were:

- As the role of governments diminishes and the freedom to businesses increases in India and everywhere in the world (with the decline of socialism and the advance of capitalism), are there any additional responsibilities business firms must take on that go beyond their narrow role of producing wealth for their shareholders?
- How will businesses earn the trust of society?
- What are the best measures to judge the performance of business managers?
- Can the business of business be only business?

What followed from these questions was the realisation that the model of a successful business that had become prevalent in the 1990s, particularly in the USA, should be re-examined and that another model may have to be developed. The challenge for leaders who would lead this development, however, is that until analysts and the media adopt new measures to judge the health and contribution of a business, these leaders will be judging themselves by measures that others around them do not use. It would be as if they and others were looking at different clocks that are not synchronised while trying to agree about the time of day.

Combining quantities and qualities

From the broad subject of business and society, Sandel brought the participants at Aspen closer to their homes and families when he asked them to read Arlie Hochschild's article, 'The Nanny Chain', in *The American Prospect,* dated January 2000. Hochschild reports the story of a college-educated schoolteacher from the Philippines who migrated to the USA to work as a housekeeper and nanny for the two-year-old son of a wealthy Beverley Hills' family where both parents were working. She loved the American boy she was caring for but missed her own children whom she had left behind in the Philippines. Perhaps here was an example of the benefits of globalisation. A woman from a poorer country could tap into the incomes of rich people in the USA and provide money for her family back home. The Americans become richer since both parents earn. The American GDP rises since the mother's income is included in the measurement of the size of the economy. At the same time, the Philippines' economy is also boosted by the remittances the maid sends home for her family. From an economist's perspective this is a win-win situation for both families and both countries.

However, the case raised many moral issues. The American participants were indignant. Was the Filipino mother correct to deprive her children of their mother's presence in order to earn money for the family? The Indians asked, what about the American mother who was working and earning and leaving her child behind with a nanny? Who is the guilty party here—the American who pays and thereby tempts a woman away from her child or the Filipino who chooses to stay away from her child so that she can earn for the family? An American CEO, a male, said he had the solution. The American family must provide the Filipino woman with at least a month's paid vacation and airfare to visit her family every year. To which another American CEO, a female, replied that she had a maid from South America, and that she was paying her to visit her family every year but the maid had requested for money in lieu of the trip home so that she could put her son through college!

So here was a case of a good economic model clashing with a model of a good family and the role of the mother in it. It was evident from the confused and emotional statements from the participants that they were having cognitive difficulty with the 'cross-model conversation' inside their own heads. The two models were hard to reconcile. Which shall yield to the other? In our analogy of clocks and the time, it is as if there are two different ways of knowing what the time really is. For the economic model we have a clock that measures the state of affairs quantitatively. But we do not have an agreed model (or clock) to assess and measure the goodness of a family. Since we have a bias towards objectivity, along with reliance on measurements and instruments, it is not surprising that the more precise clock influences our behaviours. Therefore financial measures of family income and the GDP of the nation will overpower the fuzzy assessments of the happiness of the family and the country.

The inadequacy of the models we use to diagnose the health of complex systems arises from an inability to combine quantitatively measurable and qualitatively perceptible factors into a single model. Families, business organisations, and nations are complex systems whose well-being, as we have discussed, lies in a combination of quantifiable economic factors as well as other factors that are hard to measure in monetary terms. Similarly, individual human beings are also an example of a complex system. The overall health and happiness of a human being arises from a combination of economic, psychological, and spiritual factors. Unfortunately, we tend to leave out from our scientific equations those qualities that we cannot quantify. Therefore, while the results of the equations may be precise, our calculations are fundamentally flawed. Hence, we have to learn how to combine the science of quantities with the science of qualities, thereby developing more holistic and accurate models to create the clocks that will tell us the truth that we really need to know.

Conceptual emergencies

For a 100 years and more, scientists have been vigorously pursuing knowledge about the infinitely small building blocks of our world, such as subatomic particles and genes. And now little things that run out of control, threaten to destroy the world, such as the power within nuclei and germs. Hence there arose the need for a campaign by the large nations that made these discoveries to prevent such potent weapons of mass destruction from falling into the hands of tiny bands of terrorists. We live in fear of unexpected terror and violence all over the world—including the USA, India, Britain, Russia, Southeast Asia, and South America. President Bush, who is the leader of the most powerful nation the world has ever seen, has declared a war on terrorism. The North Atlantic Treaty Organization (NATO), which played a significant role in containing the threat from the 'evil Soviet empire' (in President Reagan's memorable words), is now called upon to play a key role in eliminating the threat from terrorism.

Lord George Robertson, Secretary General of NATO, pointed to some fundamental questions when he spoke to a couple hundred Americans who met in St Andrews, Scotland in July 2003. He was asked to speak on how to make NATO more effective against the backdrop of the growing American concern about the Europeans making a fair contribution to the NATO forces. Robertson's talk combined wisdom and diplomacy. When he had finished, someone raised the issue of terrorism and NATO's role in fighting it. The question turned to another, on whether the force of arms would root out terrorism or was another approach necessary. Robertson answered, like a Zen master, saying that we have a 'Conceptual Emergency', and he waved a little booklet, which he said would suggest how to find the answer to the question!

The booklet, *Ten Things to Do in a Conceptual Emergency*, was produced by the International Futures Forum. The forum is a group of 24 economists, businessmen, technologists, scientists, philosophers and artists from the UK, Europe, USA, South Africa, and India. They first met in St Andrews in April 2001. The Scottish Council Foundation and British Petroleum had invited them for an unusual purpose—to find the next Enlightenment! The first Enlightenment had served mankind well. It had developed the power of science and industry, as well as the ideas of markets and capitalism. In fact, Adam Smith, often cited as a founder of capitalism, was born not far from St Andrews. The sponsors of the forum felt that the first Enlightenment ideas were inadequate to address the systemic problems the world was facing, such as the degradation of the environment, depletion of fresh water resources, endemic poverty in many parts of the world, and violent conflicts. In their words,

Our knowledge about the world is unprecedented, as is the level of communication across the globe, the pace of develop-ment of new technologies, and many other phenomena. In consequence, almost everywhere we look what used to be the stuff of dreams can now be contemplated in terms of practical reality. Whether or not we decide to do it, we know how to clone a human being, how to prolong human life, how to feed the world. We are living in a world in which almost anything seems possible, yet in which the forces of fragmentation and alienation seem at least as strong as those of integration and mindfulness: we seem short of the wisdom to choose which possibilities to explore and which to deny. (From *Ten Things to Do in a Conceptual Emergency.*)

After two years and four intense meetings in Scotland, the group humbly admitted it did not have the answers. The only enlightenment it could provide was a way for people to think together to understand the world better. That is what the little booklet was about. The 24 experts were like the wise men that a king had commissioned in ancient, pre-Enlightenment times to go out into the world and find the eternal truth. They returned many years later, older and wiser, to tell the king that they could offer him no eternal truth other than 'And this too shall pass'.

The booklet offers a way in which these experts from many disciplines learned to create something together after their early, very painful, 'cross-model' debates; a way to put their heads and hearts together; to combine their perspectives rather than argue about who was right and who was wrong; and thus perceive the Missing Elephant in the familiar tale of the blind men. Amongst the 10 things to do are: 'Give up the myth of control', 'Trust subjective experience', and 'Sustain networks of hope'. These were some of the major shifts in their own orientation that the 24 now humbler and wiser experts admitted.

Let us consider four examples of conceptual challenges the world is facing.

I. Challenges to the business of business

One challenge, mentioned earlier, concerns the role and regulation of businesses and markets in the development of healthy societies. This is playing out in many arenas today—in healthcare, in electricity and other utilities, and in environmental pollution. Unfortunately, the discussion tends to degenerate too soon into a clash of ideologies between so-called capitalists and socialists, supported by their respective lobbies. One has the power of money to lobby with, while the other calls on the masses to the streets.

Perhaps this conceptual challenge cannot be separated from some others that follow.

II. Perils within the system of democracy

Another conceptual challenge concerns the principles of good governance in a democracy. The concept of democracy is implemented in practice by allowing the will of the majority to prevail. A simple and, prima facie, elegant idea. But problems arise when the decisions of the majority lead to minorities being deprived of their liberty, their right to practice their own ways, and, in the extreme, even their physical security. One is often reminded that it was a majority that elected Hitler. More recently, the incumbent Chief Minister in the state of Gujarat in India, whom many blamed for the communal riots in which thousands of Muslims were killed, was re-elected with more votes shortly afterwards. He claimed that this vindicated him because in a democracy what the majority want must prevail. On the other hand, in the United Nations, the system of democracy as the will of the majority breaks down whenever the views of the majority, which includes many economically and militarily underdeveloped nations, goes against the views of a powerful minority.

In his thought-provoking book, *The Future of Freedom: Illiberal Democracy at Home and Abroad,* Fareed Zakaria, analyses several problems with the prevailing concept of democracy. He believes that it is a mistake to put blind faith in the efficacy of democracy and points out that over the past 50 years almost every economic success story in the developing world has taken place under an authoritarian regime. Zakaria's solution to the problems of democracy is a plea to the majority to delegate upwards, and give more authority to their leaders and to experts. For example, he would like central banks to become more powerful and judges to have more power and independent standing.

While considering Zakaria's proposed improvements to the practice of democracy, we may heed the caution of the judge of the Supreme Court of India who steered the path-breaking decision of the court declaring that all public service vehicles in India's polluted capital must be converted to the cleaner CNG (compressed natural gas). This resulted in a dramatic improvement of Delhi's atmosphere. But it also dislocated life in the city for months. The judge wondered if the dislocation and hardship could have been avoided by anticipating the unintended consequences of the court's ruling. Unfortunately, the court was flying blind, he said. The adversarial debate before the court between the many parties involved—citizen groups, bus manufacturers, and others—could not illuminate a comprehensive model of the situation. The court felt compelled to act even though it did not have the insights required.

The point the judge makes is that people with authority to decide often require inputs from several other people before they act. The prevalent processes to obtain these inputs and synthesise them are not very effective. Opinion polls, though quick, cannot provide the dialogue amongst contending views that is required to understand a complicated issue. And adversarial debates, whether on public platforms or in courts, create a win-lose situation that is not conducive to an open-minded understanding of contentious issues. Therefore, we have to conceive another way for the effective participation of many in decision-making.

People must have trust in the experts and elected officials to whom they delegate the right to decide on their behalf. Trust requires confidence that those being trusted will not damage us, either to further their own interests, or even unwittingly because they do not understand the complexity of the problems.

We would not trust surgeons to operate on our hearts if we doubted their competence or their interest in our well-being. Hence, while legal structures such as the design of corporate boards and constitutions of nations have a role in preventing those in power from misusing it; they cannot by themselves engender trust. Trust arises from an understanding between the parties to a contract, whether written or not, where each knows what really matters to the other and what drives their behaviours. Therefore, to build and maintain trust, a meaningful dialogue about goals and values is necessary.

III. Wars without violence

The third example of a conceptual challenge, and the one that George Robertson was alluding to, is the means by which we will create a new world order that is free of violence. The way to prevent violence, which the powerful nations of the world have used in practice, is to threaten or to use violence. NATO and the Soviets played the balance of power game for half a century, during which they developed and amassed larger piles of ever more lethal weapons. The war against terrorism is also a game of threat and counter-threat of violence. The prevailing concept, or theory-in-use, to eliminate threats of violence in the world seems to be 'an eye for an eye'. But as Mahatma Gandhi said, if we follow this concept too far, soon we will all be blind.

Here again arises the issue of trust. If we do not understand how the other party thinks, and if we cannot trust that the other party will not hurt us, whether willingly or unwittingly, we will have to keep up our defences. Seeing the size of our defences, the other party knows they are not trusted. And they fear what we may do with our strength. So they build up their defences as well. We all pile up the means of destruction and further enhance our fear of the consequences if such means were to be used!

Science and technology are rapidly marching on. Along with amazing medicines and means of communication, science is also providing us the means to destroy the world. But science cannot give us the wisdom to prevent it from happening. We have the means to reach the moon and way beyond. And very soon we will be able to reengineer human beings. But we do not yet have the means to determine what we should do with these capabilities. The wisdom that we need to understand and shape the world cannot lie within the narrow view of the world of an expert in a special discipline, be it physics or economics. We must find a better, albeit non-scientific way to take advantage of our scientific prowess and create a better world. Bombs are ticking in many parts of the world. We must find a way to defuse them soon.

IV. Many perspectives: One clock

The world is fast sailing into the new millennium. The consensus amongst economists is that the journey will make the world richer in monetary terms. The global GDP would go up. And the GDP of almost all nations of the world would show an upward trend. Seen through this economic lens, and judged by a monetary measure, there is nothing to fear for the future. However, many fear that this strongly held but narrow (and hence, in its own way, fundamentalist) view of progress does not give enough importance to the quality of diversity that will make for a richer world. Many fear that the relentless march on this narrow road, focussed on economic growth through globalisation, is threatening diversity. They would like a world with multiple modernities and not just one Western and increasingly US-centric view of what it means to be modern.

The challenge before the world is to respect, grow, and take advantage of the multiple modern sensibilities each with its own roots, both in the East and West. A group of international scholars who met in 2002 in 'search of a new paradigm for a sustainable human order' (in their words) heard pleas from several of their members for a world with many paradigms, and not just one. The proceedings of this group's meeting are reported in the journal, *World Affairs* (January-March 2003). The desire to have a multiplicity of modernities, civilisations, or paradigms developing side by side may have aesthetic motivations. A world with variety will be a more interesting place with more to see and learn about than a world that is uniform. The desire for preserving multiple ways may also have moral compulsions, rooted in the liberal idea of protecting the rights of all individuals and minorities. There may be even a practical reason to have variety, which is to stimulate ongoing innovation and progress. The clash, combination, and mutation of ideas produce innovation. We seem to realise the need, whether for aesthetic or practical reasons, for rich ecologies that have a great variety of forms. Therefore we urge the preservation of rain forests and wetlands. And we say that the quality of its melting pot with many people and their talents explains the ferment of ideas and change in the USA, keeping it ahead of other countries.

There seem to be many benefits in retaining a multiplicity of views. But how can we understand each other in this Tower of Babel, with its multiple modernities, civilisations and paradigms? Moreover, as we come closer by communication, trade, and economic necessity into one increasingly connected world, financial contagion, terror, and diseases move easily across the world. Therefore, along with multiple cultures and paradigms, we also seem to need a unifying worldview with which we can govern the world for the safety of all. We must not permit anyone to use violence to impose their views on others. But many do not have much patience with the alternative way, that of democratic discourse.

Therefore, our fourth conceptual challenge is to develop effective processes of governance for a world with diversity: to preserve many models and yet create one unifying model. In this richly diverse yet unified world, how will we conduct effective 'cross-model' conversations between people from different cultures and different academic and scientific disciplines? What should be the design of the clock that can guide a collection of people who also have clocks of their own set differently? And how will this clock be developed? This in itself is a conceptual and practical challenge, and is the challenge that this book is addressing.

Evolving an Idea for India

There is no other country with as much diversity that has been as committed to democracy since its inception as India. Therefore, models of management of the economy that may apply in less heterogeneous or less democratic societies cannot be transposed into India. India has to find its own solutions to fit its needs

A first division in every subject, yet placed in the third division overall! If your child brought home such a report card you would think there was something wrong with the examiners. Last year India performed in the first division in global competition for exports, investments, and growth. It was in the top quartile in rankings of countries in terms of GDP growth, merchandise exports, service exports, and FDI inflows, and also in a survey of confidence of international investors. Yet, in two widely cited surveys of country competitiveness—that of the World Economic Forum (WEF) and the Swiss Institute of Management Development—India was rated in the third division (the third quartile) in terms of factors that make a country competitive! What is the credibility of reports that say a country does not

Article first published in *The Economic Times*.

have what it takes to compete when it is actually competing very well? Clearly there is something wrong with the underlying model—the combination of factors that make a country competitive—used in these reports. Therefore let us not be overly impressed with the sizes of the samples and the precision of the numbers in the opinion polls masquerading as research in such reports. They cannot tell us what we really need to know to improve our competitiveness further. We have to look deeper.

But I am not going to delve into the concept of competitiveness. I want to go even deeper, into the conceptual vacuum inside many reports and seminars about development, competitiveness, and growth. The reports attract us with their glossiness, and the seminars with the glitterati of the attendance list which is their main, and often, only attraction. 'Conceptually deficient debates' was how the economic adviser to one of the world's largest investment banks described such seminars. He was commenting, at the time, on the anxious debate in the financial press and in business seminars in the USA and Europe about the weakness of the US dollar. But he could have been describing seminars in New Delhi about India's competitiveness and development.

Setting the stage for the WEF-CII India Economic Summit in November 2002, an economist said at the opening plenary that India has four challenges to improve its competitiveness: ecological sustainability, social equity, federalism with unity, and managing diversity. He went on to say that the driving forces in the now dominant, free-market paradigm of development were greed and self-interest. If people consume more and more, to catch up with and have more than their neighbours, economies will grow. The four challenges he named are the consequences of the two driving forces that are being let loose without the guidance of any higher ideology. However, none at the meeting, not even the economist himself, would go further to seriously question the prevalent ideology of economic progress for fear that they could be quickly branded as archaic Gandhian idealists or left-over socialists and ostracised for spoiling the party just when it started to swing.

The world is facing a 'conceptual emergency', according to the provocative expression of the International Futures Forum. We need better concepts with which to govern globalisation, the development of countries, and the management of corporations if we want to create a better world for the future. But we are not willing or able to find these concepts. Many are not willing to question prevalent orthodoxy for fear of being branded as grass chewers and banished to the outer regions of the debate where they can fulminate in the cold while the inner circle hears each other's speeches within warmly bedecked halls.

I am not a certified economist. I study how organisations and societies learn and implement new ideas, especially transformational ideas. Such ideas are much more difficult to learn and implement than ideas of new products and new techniques. Because these big ideas generally challenge the passionately held fundamental beliefs of people—for example, the ideas that free markets are the best way to organise a society, or that managed economies grow faster. Organisations and societies adopt new ideas through a process of conflict and experimentation. It is a messy process. It takes time. And sometimes it fails. My quest is to find the way in which this process of learning can be faster and more effective.

I am concerned that we must very soon discover and act on a way for India to grow at over 8 per cent per annum. Too many young people's futures and too many poor people's hopes are waiting on this. Our pride as a viable and secure nation that counts amongst the pantheon of nations is also at stake. It is dawning on me that no economist anywhere in the world yet knows the way to produce a sustainable change in our trajectory. And I doubt that the approach many are taking to find the answer can really work out. Therefore we have to change the way we are going about finding the solution.

Clearly, the experts at the World Bank and International Monetary Fund (IMF), who had the privilege of overseeing the development of many countries, do not have the answer. They are busy proving each other wrong. Maybe one should not expect them to have the answer yet. After all the idea of managed economic development emerged only after the Second World War. It is a fairly new idea as HW Arndt points out in *Economic Development: The History of an Idea*. New strategies for the sustainable growth of nations and organisations cannot be validated in a hurry. We are easily intrigued by something different that begins to succeed and jump hastily to the conclusion that it is a sustainable solution. In his book, *Just Capital: The Liberal Economy*, Adair Turner lists the many wonders of economic growth extolled by economists in the last 30 years. They include, in chronological order, the German wonder, the Japanese miracle, the Asian tigers, the New Economy, US style free markets, and now China. We are still searching, he says.

In our search for an idea for India we may be looking in the wrong places. I remember a conversation in the 1960s with the head of Singapore's Economic Development Board. He had invited the Tatas to help Singapore. I asked him what he expected to learn from the Tatas when many more advanced Western firms were coming to Singapore. He said, 'What they know, and what we can see is what they are doing now. They have even forgotten what they did when they were at our stage of development. We have to find more relevant examples, and not be dazzled by others' superior situations.' He was a wise man. We must not confuse the results achieved by the societies we admire with what they did to get those results. For example, we admire the framework of property rights in the USA. But we cannot transplant it in a developing country. We should ask what was the process of its evolution. We may be surprised to find the legitimisation of encroachments on land in the USA in the nineteenth century whereby capital was put into the hands of poor people. These are the 'missing lessons of US history' described by Hernando de Soto in *The Mystery of Capital: Why Capitalism Triumphs in the West and Fails Everywhere Else.*

Moreover, no two complex situations are the same. Neustadt and May of the Kennedy School of Government give several instructive stories in *Thinking in Time: The Uses of History for Decision Makers* regarding how policy-makers have caused unintended damage by transferring ideas from settings that are not suited to the essential features of their own situation. There are three essential conditions of our situation in India that have never existed in this combination for any country. Our starting points are:

- We are a poor country with a huge population.
- We have great diversity.
- And we are (and wish to remain) a democracy.

With these three conditions, we want to grow fast. Everytime one considers emulating another country, whether Singapore, Chile, the USA, or China, one or other of these three conditions appears as an obstacle. Therefore we have to do what has not been done before. We have to develop our own idea of rapid development. And, more importantly, we need to develop it in a way that it will be acted upon.

The most critical know-how that India must develop if it wants accelerated economic development is the ability to evolve an innovative approach that is well suited to our conditions. And we will have to develop this through a participative process that takes advantage of our diversity. This is not a problem of economics. It is a problem of societal learning and of leadership during that process of learning.

The improvement of India's competitiveness, an acceleration in its development, and the elimination of poverty are inter-related and vitally important subjects that deserve a deeper dialogue amongst leaders from the trinity of business, government, and civil society. Many feel the need for an Indian model that builds on our value systems, that is related to our current reality, and also takes advantage of knowledge available in other countries. But this model cannot emerge from 'conceptually deficient debates'. Therefore, leaders will have to work together in 'off the record' dialogues without 'prepared remarks', and systematically struggle through the intellectual and emotional confusion that is the pain of delivering a new idea.

Splash Around the Benefits of Growth

Strategies for India's economic development must spread the creation of jobs and fix India's unique position in the global economy

'It is not the economy, stupid: it's the jobs!' That was the lesson from the last US presidential election. Globalisation and free trade are nice to espouse, but local jobs matter most. The US economy is recovering, corporate profits are growing, but growth is not translating into jobs. 'All politics is local,' said Tip O'Neil, former Speaker of the US Congress. Therefore, the Democrats are railing against outsourcing to India and even against 'Benedict Arnold' companies in the USA that let down local people to make more profits for shareholders. Meanwhile, incumbent Republicans are saved perhaps by an external threat to national security.

If jobs matter in the USA, they matter even more in India— perhaps more than any other country. India has the largest youth population in the world. About 34 per cent of India's

Article first published in *The Economic Times*.

population is less than 15 years old, higher than China (25 per cent) and the USA (21 per cent). Most of these 350 million young Indians will need jobs in the next two decades. A sustained growth in GDP is essential to create jobs. Goldman Sachs calculates that India will become the third largest economy in the world by 2050. But growth cannot be taken for granted: India needs the strategies to achieve it. And the pattern of growth must spread incomes and jobs throughout India's vast population, because its polity will be less tolerant than the USA's with growth that does not create jobs. Growth in India must 'splash around' (borrowing a phrase from *The Economist*) because there may not be the time for it to trickle down.

Strategies to achieve this imperative emerge from two unique aspects of India's position within global demographics. One of these is well known. The proportion of the working age people to total population is declining in all developed countries, due to lower birth rates and increase in life expectancy. India, however, will have the opposite problem, of too many working age people. In fact, the surplus in India by 2020 is expected to be 47 million people, against a shortfall of 17 million in the USA and 10 million in China. The other countries with large surpluses are Pakistan (17 million) and Bangladesh (10 million). Amongst these countries with large surpluses, India's professionally qualified workforce stands out, a result of the country's post-independence policies focussing on the need to promote higher education and create industrial capabilities in many fields.

The other unprecedented development is that whereas all rich countries in terms of GDP have hitherto also had high per capita incomes, India will remain a relatively poor country in terms of per capita income even when it has been predicted to be the third largest economy in the world in terms of GDP in 2050. India's GDP will become huge because India will have an enormous population that will keep growing until 2050.

But the per capita income in India will remain about one-fourth of that of other large economies such as the USA, Japan, and the richer countries of Europe. This has two implications. The first is that Indian labour costs will remain competitive until 2050. The second is that, on average, Indians will not be able to afford the same prices for products (in currency conversion terms) as citizens of other large economies. Therefore, to tap into the power of India's huge market, products and services will have to suit the purchasing power and tastes of the millions of emerging customers in India. Multinationals that have tried to sell products that have been basically designed for richer countries have already been frustrated in India, and those that wait for the Indian masses to attain the same levels of incomes as people in other developed countries will miss the profits they could gather while the Indian economy grows.

These conditions suggest three broad strategies for India. They are not imitations of the FDI-led mass manufacturing and coastal-enclave-based strategies China used to spur its remarkable growth. China took advantage of opportunities available to it, as India should now do. First, demographic trends as well as the swift growth of the Internet and communications technology in the last decade give India a special position in the global knowledge economy. China did not have this possibility when it took off. India should strengthen its position as a service hub for the world with the capability to provide knowledge-based services in many fields as well as manufactured products that have a high skill content. To sustain its competitive advantage, India must increase the dynamism and reach of its professional and vocational education systems. Add inward tourism, where India's potential is barely tapped, to outward knowledge services, and the latent potential of services to boost employment in India can be realised.

The second strategy is to develop a large internal market for manufactured products, while taking advantage of the low production costs within India. Restraints on the manufacturing sector, such as cumbersome labour regulations, must continue to be eased. And hindrances to interstate commerce within India may need to be removed. With a boost from such policy changes, and innovations in their own products and distribution strategies, presently small Indian manufacturers can acquire large scales by serving the Indian market, and become stronger to compete internationally.

Third, India must develop its rural/agricultural economy. For incomes to rapidly spread around rather than trickle down, for employment to be provided to India's masses of which 70 per cent live in rural areas or for urban blight to be minimised; India should develop a model of growth that stimulates productive economic activity in rural areas. Villages must be connected with better roads and telecommunications, and local entrepreneurship must be stimulated. Rural roads and telecommunications are now receiving the attention of policy-makers. And innovative business models are emerging. While these examples give hope, there is concern about 'scaling up' of the ideas. But this may be the wrong metaphor. What is required, rather, is to 'spread around' the ideas and thus generate a million fireflies of change that can bring life and light to the darkness in the interiors so people do not have to rush to the bright lights of the cities.

Will all this add up to the same proportions of services, manufacturing, and agriculture that other countries had when they were at our stage of 'development'? Perhaps not, but it does not matter, because effective strategies always fit specific starting conditions and objectives. These strategies fit our conditions and should produce the results that we wish to achieve.

6

New
Ways

No, sir, this is neither a flood-hit nor a drought-hit area. We are only hit by bad government!

6

New Ways

Ah, when to the heart of man
Was it ever less than a treason
To go with the drift of things,
To yield with a grace to reason

—Robert Frost, 'Reluctance'

SHARED aspirations inspire people (and also bind teams). The concepts and models at the back of our minds influence what we pay attention to and shape our thoughts. And our thoughts guide our actions which, at the end of the day produce results. Thus, passion, concepts, and skills together produce great results.

If you want to play the sitar as well as Ravi Shankar you must know how to handle the sitar and pluck the strings with the adeptness he displays. Similarly, if you want to bowl like Anil Kumble you have to learn to grip the ball properly and to swing your arm and wrist in order to make the ball do what you want it to. But plucking strings and handling the cricket ball is not all you need to learn. Ravi Shankar has a way of bringing out the flow of notes that makes his music special. Similarly, Kumble has a way of determining the best combination of line, length, and spin of ball that makes him very dangerous to batsmen. Clearly, they both have a concept or strategy in their heads that is different and more effective than other sitar players and bowlers who may have similar dexterity in their hands. Therefore, to play like Ravi Shankar or Kumble, one has to learn their concepts as well. But even that is not sufficient. These masters also play with a passion that makes their performances truly great. Their passion and their concepts can be sensed but cannot be observed explicitly, whereas the way the maestros use their fingers can. It is easier to observe and imitate what is visible. But by limiting learning merely to what is visible, one will miss the essence of their great performances.

These two examples examine the passion, art, and skill of individual performers. Could there be a similar pattern within high performing organisations? Let us consider three examples.

Concepts and actions—What we believe and therefore what we do

By the early 1980s the world had realised that something unusual had happened in Japan in the previous 20 years. Japanese TVs, radios, watches, cameras, machines, cars, and steel were sweeping through the world. Their prices were much lower than those of American and European products. The surprise was that their quality and performance was much better. Japanese companies had broken the compromise of quality and costs. The ingrained belief of managers elsewhere was that better quality must require higher costs. The Japanese turned this notion on its head. They established that actually it is poor quality that creates more cost. Japanese companies also overturned another hoary concept of manufacturing management, that more stocks must be kept to ensure timely supplies. Their factories were reputed to store hardly any parts, and yet always delivered products on time.

Sumant Moolgaokar, passed on to me an invitation from a Japanese organisation to visit Japan, to meet Dr Ishikawa, who had spearheaded the quality drive in the Japanese industry along with Dr Deming. Visits to the factories of Toyota, Nissan, Matsushita, Hitachi, and NEC as well as meetings with senior executives of these companies were also arranged. At that time, very little was known about how the Japanese had achieved their breakthrough. Naturally, I was delighted that Moolgaokar was willing to sponsor me and pay the hefty fee.

The highlight of the trip for the group of 30 executives from all over the world was the visit to Toyota's factory in Nagoya. Toyota was the fountainhead of ideas that had changed the fundamental concepts of manufacturing management. The factory was unlike automobile factories in America and Europe. It was clean, compact, and quiet. There were hardly any stocks of parts. And it hummed along uninterrupted. Later, we assembled in a conference room to hear the head of Toyota's industrial engineering division, which had invented the famous 'Toyota Production System', explain the principles of the system to us. He spoke in Japanese, through an interpreter. In words that sounded like poetry, rather than the complex jargon of management, he explained the elegant simplicity of the system. With his explanation it became obvious to most of us why the Toyota system could achieve the startling performance we had seen, whereas factories elsewhere, working with a different logic, could not do so.

When the talk was over, an American executive had a question. 'Can we see a sample of the computer form you use for your production control system?' he asked. His concept of inventory management was better computer systems. His company was known to be investing millions of dollars in state-of-the-art systems. Therefore, he believed that if Toyota was doing so well it must have an outstanding computer system. The rest of us were surprised that he should ask such a question. Not only had we seen no evidence of computers in the factory, but with the explanation of the underlying logic of Toyota's system, we could now understand why complicated calculations were not required. The Toyota executive replied, that the production control form was in the folder that had already been given to us. The American executive pulled out the simple little form—the now universally known 'kanban' card. He was incredulous that such a simple and concise form could provide the information required to keep inventories under control. He turned to the visitors sitting beside him and murmured, 'The Japanese never tell the real truth, do they?'

I was sorry that the American executive had not at all understood the concept of the Toyota system that was so beautifully explained to us. His own concept of manufacturing management was so ingrained in his mind that he could not accept evidence of the fact that there may be another, very different, way. The Toyota executive had eloquently explained to the visitors, who had come to understand the Japanese miracle, that a core concept of the Toyota system was that inventory has to be eliminated, and not managed. Toyota believed that inventory in the factory was like a carpet under which many evils could be hidden. If the carpet is removed, there is nowhere for the problems to hide: Problems of machine performance for example, or variation in quality. These have to be tackled because the production will stop if there is a problem. And people will have to find a solution to the problem to ensure it does not arise again. Thus the performance capability of the manufacturing process is improved.

When Toyota shook up the automobile industry with its startling results and its new approach to manufacturing, General Motors, the largest company in the world, took notice. General Motors sent people to find out what Toyota was doing. They came back with what they could observe, that was radically different in what Toyota did. For example, Toyota's factories were clean. Painted stripes on the floors demarcated aisles and areas for storage. Also, the people seemed to work well with each other. They all wore uniforms, and did callisthenics and sang the company song together every morning. General Motors, and many other American companies, quickly replicated these visible practices. Unfortunately, the performance of their factories did not improve. They had missed the underlying concepts of manufacturing organisation that Toyota applied, and in which lay the real power of its innovation in production.

A concept in Toyota that was fundamentally different to factories in the West was that workmen on the shop floor were responsible for improving quality. They were trained to solve quality problems and given the required time and a place on the factory floor to meet and solve them. In the West until then, quality improvement was the job of trained staff engineers who worked out solutions and issued revised operating procedures whenever required, and production supervisors ensured that workmen followed them. Deeper examination would have shown the American managers who came in looking for new ideas that teamwork amongst workmen in Japan was induced far more by the 'quality circles' in which they worked together on the shop floor than through the songs they sang together in the mornings.

Different concepts require different procedures for execution. For example, a Japanese factory that does not keep inventories would not require sophisticated processes and routines for managing inventories. It would, however, require good processes and techniques for effective problem solving by workmen since it relies on them for performance improvement. In contrast, a Western factory, working with different concepts would need more investment in tools for inventory management than for training workmen in quality. Thus we can understand why the American executive at Toyota, with a different concept ingrained in his mind, was looking for the tools for inventory management, whereas for many others, including myself, the light bulb had lit up—tools for training and involving workmen with quality improvement were required to achieve low levels of inventory!

Another example of the power of concepts to shape our thoughts and actions arose from a study by the International Council of Executive Development Research (ICEDR) based in the USA. ICEDR carried out an extensive research in the mid-1990s with over 2000 senior executives in multinational corporations (MNCs) all over the world. Its researchers wanted to know what was these executives' greatest challenge. After very systematic distillation of the replies, the answer was: the creation of an organisation that is very stable and yet very changeable; that is efficient yet innovative; and that has the benefits of a global scale and is yet locally responsive. These executives wanted to have seemingly opposing qualities in the same organisation: predictability and stability on the one hand, and change-ability and creativity on the other. A question that arises is why do these qualities seem to be in opposition? Could the problem be with the fundamental concept of how business organisations are run, and could the application of another concept dissolve this dilemma (just as Toyota's new concept of manufacturing had dissolved hitherto unsolvable dilemmas in manufacturing management)?

The language that managers use when they talk about their organisations illuminates the dominant metaphor that drives their thinking: 'Reengineering'; organisation 'structure' (invariably a pyramidal construction of boxes and lines); 'levers' to pull to make change happen; first detailed design and then execution (implementation of the design). Evidently they think of their organisations as machines. The problem with machines is that they are designed and put together by an agency that is external to them, and they therefore do not have the change-ability within them. Mechanical engineers are familiar with the second law of thermodynamics which states that the entropy (loosely equivalent to disorder and consequent reduction in capability) of any closed system must increase over time. That is exactly what happens to machines. However, another equally valid law of science says that the capability of complex systems increases over time. This is the law of evolution that applies to biological systems. Therefore if business organisations could be designed in accordance with principles of biological systems, perhaps they could have an inherent ability to continuously adapt and evolve with the demands of the environment, an ability that the executives in the survey aspired to build.

In hindsight, Telco was able to respond so magnificently to the threat of the Japanese companies in India, in the story of Project Jupiter I have mentioned earlier, because the human resource systems of Telco in Pune were designed with a biological metaphor, and in fact a gardening metaphor, in mind. Telco's vision was to create a learning factory that would develop new capabilities as it grew. The human resource systems were radically different from those in Telco's first factory in Jamshedpur that had been established with Daimler Benz' assistance. In Jamshedpur, the tasks to be performed by every workman were specified in detail within the design of every production process. Workmen were, in effect, the extensions of machines. They were paid incentives to work faster to improve the output of the machines. This was the standard industrial engineering approach followed in most factories all over the world. The problem with this approach was that whenever the process had to be changed to introduce a new product or to introduce a better machine, the tasks to be performed by the workmen and the incentives to be paid to them had to be renegotiated. There was also little incentive for workmen to improve their capabilities because the number of vacancies determined by the industrial engineering department controlled capability-related promotions. Bargaining was required to change production rates and to create new vacancies; unions were involved; and this delayed the introduction of new products and technical processes.

The approach in Pune was fundamentally different. If people were indeed the only appreciating assets in the organisation, and could improve their own capabilities and also make improvements in the production processes, then they should be managed accordingly and not as components of technical processes designed by engineers. Because if they were, then the second law of thermodynamics would inevitably apply over time, as it had in Jamshedpur. The 'entropy' in the organisation had built up there. The organisation had become internally entangled in disputes between workmen, managers, industrial engineers, and unions. And thus they had become more resistant to change.

In Pune, people were considered as seeds that have latent capabilities. The gardener can only create conditions for the seeds to grow. He/she waters and fertilises the seed, and removes weeds and pests. But he/she cannot pull the shoots out of the seeds. Therefore, conditions were created in Pune where workmen would want to grow. They were paid according to their capabilities and skills. Facilities as well as incentives were provided to learn. Workmen could apply for a higher wage if they acquired a new capability. They were tested rigorously. If they passed, they got an increase in salary. There were no limitations on the numbers of individuals who could thus earn higher salaries by expanding their capabilities. The strategic concept underlying this approach was that the more skilled and versatile the workforce, the faster the company would be able to make improvements in production processes, and also new product development would emerge faster. Telco benefited immensely from this human resource strategy when the Japanese truck manufacturers arrived in India. Telco developed a new truck in 18 months, whereas the fastest time in the world then was between three and four years. The versatility of the workforce enabled deployment of people from many departments to activities on the critical path, such as the production of a working prototype, which was completed in just over a month. Thus Telco was able to convincingly beat back the Japanese challenge in India.

Aspirations and concepts—What we want, and how it can change what we believe

A good example of the effect of aspiration on change in imbedded concepts (or mindsets) is provided by Toyota and the Japanese industry in general. A strong force driving the learning in Japanese factories was the desire to make Japan the global leader in industry. In his lecture to the foreign executives visiting Japan to study Japanese quality management that I referred to earlier, Dr Ishikawa, the guru of the Japanese quality movement, described how Japanese people, defeated in the Second World War, yearned to prove that they were as good as the best. This theme was repeated in discussions with executives in several companies, including Toyota when they were asked how the quality movement began.

Another example is the turnaround of Harley-Davidson, the American motorcycle company that had been almost beaten into the ground by Honda and Yamaha. The turnaround of the company under its CEO Richard Teerlink's inspiring leadership is a legend in the annals of management. The company reengineered its supply chain and production process, and it totally changed its marketing strategy. I had an unforgettable meeting with Teerlink in his office. At the outset of the meeting I asked him what was the key to the turnaround? He said it was the willingness to break out of old mindsets. 'What was the key to unlock the mind?' I asked. 'It is the vision of success in the minds of everyone—the vision of shaping a very special company,' he said. 'And what precisely was that vision?' I asked. 'Oh, it is not what the vision is,' he said. 'It is what a vision does that matters.' He told me that a journalist was visiting Harley-Davidson that day. The journalist had inquired whether all employees knew the vision statement of Harley-Davidson. Teerlink had told the journalist to go out and meet as many people in the factory as he wanted and find out for himself. Teerlink was expecting him back in a few minutes. 'Why don't you wait and hear him?' he suggested. Soon the journalist came into the room. 'So, how many employees know the vision statement?' Teerlink asked. 'Actually no one knew the words of the statement, Mr Teerlink', he replied. 'But it is amazing how well they understand the spirit of it. And I must say that I have never seen people so zestful and so curious about new ideas in any other factory that I have visited,' he said. Teerlink confirmed that the change in thought and behaviour of everyone, including himself, was a result of that spirit.

Another example of how aspiration to achieve the seemingly impossible can spur innovations in thought and action is the story of the turnaround of Tatab Industries in Malaysia that I have told in an earlier chapter. It ended with a Japanese manager applauding the capabilities of an Indian management team that had just beaten his Japanese team. The story started with the discovery of a shared aspiration amongst the Indian team to prove that they were the best in the world. But aspiration was not enough to win. New ideas were necessary. Tatab Industries could not reduce its losses unless it could sell more trucks and buses. But merely selling more would not be enough. The price had to be high as well. Calculations showed that it would have to be higher than the prices of Japanese vehicles though it could be below the Mercedes price.

A sales strategy emerged by understanding the aspirations of the potential customers. At that time, customers of trucks and buses in Malaysia were mostly Chinese owners of small businesses.

They were hardworking people who wanted to get rich quickly. They liked to drive an expensive car as soon as they could afford one to show off to their neighbours and friends. Their aspiration was to own a Mercedes car with the famous three-point star on the grill. However, very few could afford one and they envied those who could. These same people bought Mercedes trucks, making Mercedes the best selling trucks in Malaysia at that time. They said they valued the robustness of Mercedes trucks compared to the Japanese and hence were willing to pay a high price for them.

I noticed that most of these businessmen owned Toyota Corollas or other similar, small Japanese cars. Tatab's sales strategy emerged from the appreciation of the aspirations and beliefs of Tatab's potential customers. Tata trucks looked and felt like Mercedes' trucks—after all they were developed on the lines of Mercedes Benz designs. But there were two principal differences from a customer's perspective: While Tata trucks were 15 per cent cheaper than Mercedes, they did not have the famous Mercedes star on their grill! We did some simple, back-of-the-envelope calculations to show to the Chinese customers that if they bought a Tata truck rather than a Mercedes truck, they could own a Mercedes car instead of a Toyota within a year. Of course, the initial price was not the only factor to be considered. A Mercedes truck could be overloaded more than Japanese trucks and hence operators could make more money. We guaranteed that Tata trucks could be used and abused as much as the Mercedes trucks.

The sales pitch of the Tatab sales team, who were all Chinese, and could talk candidly to the Chinese buyers was, 'Be practical, man! Why do you want to pay 15 per cent more just to have a star on the grill of your truck? Get the star on your car, where your girlfriend or wife can see it. If you buy a Tata truck instead of a Mercedes, I guarantee you can sell your Corolla and buy a new Mercedes car in a year and here is how.'

Though the pitch was compelling, it was not enough. We had to prove that Tata trucks would actually make more money for the operators so they could earn in order to be able to buy their Mercedes cars. We set an internal goal within the Tatab team to ensure that the buyers of our trucks actually earned enough to buy their new Mercedes cars in a year's time. If a Tata truck had any breakdown, the service team would respond immediately, and get the truck back on the road quickly, thus earning money without losing time. Mercedes Benz had a very efficient service centre. But if a Mercedes customer with a problem showed up at one o'clock on Saturday afternoon, he would be told to return on Monday morning. We changed the rules of the game. If a customer showed up at the Tata service centre at closing time on Saturday, a service crew would stay over until his vehicle was fixed so that it could be back on the road during the weekend to earn money for its owner.

One Saturday night, the Tata Service Manager, a senior officer, was entertaining friends in his house. He received an anxious call from the Sales Manager—the same Chinese man who was alleged to have deposited the strangled body of the Service Manager's dog at his doorstep. An irate customer had called. His Tata truck, carrying a load of fresh fish from Johore Baru to Kuala Lumpur had broken down on the highway. Its rear axle shaft was broken. The Tata dealer nearby did not have a spare. The Tata service centre in Kuala Lumpur was closed. What was to be done? The truck owner was threatening that if the fish rotted, as it would if the truck could not move, he would dump the rotten fish at the Sales Manager's doorstep. The irony in the threat—dead fish and dead dog—was not lost on the Service Manager. He could let the Sales Manager stew! However, he excused himself from the party. He went to the service centre, opened it, picked up a spare shaft, and drove through the night to the broken-down truck. He was no spring chicken—he was 50 years old. Nevertheless, he rolled under the truck, and with the help of the dealer's mechanic personally replaced the shaft. The truck arrived in the morning at the fish market, just in time to sell its cargo. By word of mouth that story of service beyond the call of duty spread very fast through the truckers' community.

In the next few weeks, there was an unfortunate spate of breakdowns of rear axle shafts on Tata trucks. Obviously the customers were overloading them. The service centre ran out of spares. Replenishments from India would take weeks at the earliest. The Production Manager agreed to stop his production line in the factory and pull out shafts from finished vehicles that were ready for delivery so that the customers' vehicles could keep running and earn them money, even if it meant a loss of sales to Tatab who could not sell the new vehicles. The word was out in the market: 'The Tatas care more about their customers making money than making money for themselves; whereas Mercedes' systems, albeit very efficient, are designed to make more money for Mercedes.'

Such fundamental changes in attitudes and principles by which the Tatas' systems ran helped the Tatab team to win customers' hearts. By the end of the year, many Tata truck owners bought Mercedes cars. In fact, the Tatab salesmen helped them to negotiate better prices from Mercedes! The stories of these delighted truck owners were widely publicised. 'Be practical like me and fulfil your dreams,' they said. 'Buy a Tata truck experience. It is the best value for money.'

I am convinced that the change in systems and behaviours of the organisation, which are a reflection of new learning, would not have come about without the deeply shared aspiration of the people. That aspiration was not a statement on the wall—in fact there was no vision statement. But the vision was alive and heartfelt every day. It continued to inspire people to think of new ideas.

A very strong thread within the Learning Field ties 'Know-Wants', 'Know-Whys', 'Know-Hows', and 'Know-Whats'. Therefore, to accelerate learning and change, it is important to understand where the thread is tangled or broken and to act at these points. Very often, the points with most leverage for transformation of people's behaviour are at the level of 'Know-Wants' and 'Know-Whys'. But these are soft, squishy points, compared to the 'Know-Hows' of information and work procedures, and managers will often tend to focus on the latter because they know how to reengineer such concrete processes.

Moreover, millions of people are involved in large social systems. And there exists more diversity amongst them than large business organisations. Therefore, even if the need to align the aspirations of people is acknowledged, a practical question is, how can it be done? And, how can many diverse beliefs be reconciled? Since we do not have answers to these questions, and fear that a process of involving large numbers will take a very long time, if it can be done at all, we may be disinclined to even try.

But, before we give up, let us consider what skills we will need and what a process to develop a shared vision may look like. Perhaps it has not been done before in a country with the size and diversity of India. But, surely, in the spirit of what we have discovered so far, let us begin with an aspiration to find a solution. Then let us look at the way we presently talk and listen to each other. Maybe if we change the way we do this, we could find the solution.

Managing India: A Single
Point Plan of Action

Many people want the country's political leaders to 'get on with it' and make change happen, the way CEOs do in their organisations. However, the 'CEO' models of leadership and change management that work well in business corporations may not be the solution for change in a pluralistic democracy

Many experts are proposing solutions to address the malaise in India's economy. We have seen a spate of six-, seven-, and eight-point plans in the past and no doubt more will be proposed in the months to come. However, it is finally dawning on us that the unsatisfactory progress of India is the result of our inability to implement solutions and not the lack of knowledge regarding what the solutions are. The difficulties of implementation are also beginning to be understood. The principal difficulty is that many of the basic problems that need to be addressed—such as building infrastructure, improving productivity in businesses and governments, and rethinking

Article first published in *The Economic Times*.

user subsidies—require the cooperation of many stakeholders, some of whom have to give up benefits they have so far enjoyed. Therefore more reports by experts, no matter how well analysed and presented, will not help. We now need to work on the root cause, which is our present inadequate ability to implement solutions that involve many people with diverse interests who have to work together. This must be our single point plan of action.

We have begun to grope for solutions to the problem of implementation. Unfortunately, the way we have begun the search may have two fundamental flaws. The first flaw is the belief that the solution may lie primarily in the way successful business leaders make things happen. There is presently a great romance with the efficacy of business methods and business leaders all over the world. This leads to a temptation to apply the concepts from business to the operation of much more complex socio-economic systems such as nations. However, we must recognise the fundamental structural differences between twentieth century business corporations and twenty-first-century nations. A few years back someone said that with the fall of the Berlin Wall the last remaining totalitarian state was the Anglo-Saxon business corporation. The tough leaders of businesses can downsize their workforces in economic downturns to maintain their company's financial performance. But countries cannot throw people out when the economy slows down to maintain their growth of per capita GNP. Business leaders can acquire or merge with other companies, or sell parts of their own, to generate value for their shareholders. Whereas leaders of countries would have to risk their lives if they had proposed similar options! Business leaders are rewarded handsomely with the stock of their companies. But political leaders whose personal wealth grows faster than others in the country are an anathema in a democracy. Given these fundamental differences, we should not be simplistic in applying leadership models and processes from business to government. We should search more carefully for the solution.

The second flaw is in the manner in which business people in India are coming together to find the solution for India. For example, recently a national TV channel organised a 'managing India brainstorm' with a galaxy of business leaders to 'define the future of India'. They invited two eminent Indian scientists as well—Dr Kasturi Rangan and Dr Anji Reddy. Unfortunately, the meeting could not benefit from their insights. The discussion kept getting stuck in the problems and views of the Indian business leaders who dominated the meeting, even though the scientists repeatedly reminded the organisers that the subject of the meeting was 'managing India' and not merely the management of businesses in India! Not surprisingly, the meeting did not produce any fresh thoughts nor create any more momentum towards implementation of national solutions.

If our single point plan is to create an alignment amongst the diverse groups who must together implement solutions to India's complex problems, then we must have deeper dialogues amongst diverse stakeholders. In these dialogues, all diverse points of views must be heard carefully, not just politely tolerated. Moreover, these dialogues should not be posed as debates in which two opposing points of view are pitted against each other to determine winners and losers. We need a national consensus in which everyone can discover the benefits for themselves.

Is such a dialogue an idealistic dream? I would say it is no more a dream than is the vision of a transformed India offered by the experts if only we can implement their six-, seven-, or eight-point solutions. In fact, if we do not first make the dialogue a reality, the vision will be a castle in the air forever!

Approaches to Urban Transformation

We may want the same results that have been obtained in Singapore and Shanghai for our cities in India, but we have to use means that fit our conditions. Participative approaches that are being adopted in some Indian cities should be considered.

ABOUT 25 years ago, the transformation of Singapore amazed the world and today visitors to Shanghai are amazed at the transformation of that city. Now plans for improvement of Indian cities are in the air. An ambitious master plan has recently been prepared for Mumbai. And a process of improvement is also under way in Bangalore.

Recently I had the pleasure of hearing Nandan Nilekani, CEO of Infosys, describe the changes that were being made in Bangalore. He was exchanging thoughts with a small group of people concerned with bringing about improvements in Mumbai and Pune. Nilekani explained the reasons why, according to him, the initiative of the Bangalore Action Task Force (BATF),

---

Article first published in *The Economic Times*.

that he heads, and the associated process of Janaagraha are succeeding. These initiatives are improving various civil amenities in Bangalore. Since Nilekani is not a 'clueless head of an NGO government' (as a political analyst rather scathingly described a former Indian Chief Minister) but the CEO of one of India's most successful companies, his insights into what makes change happen deserve the attention of all those who say that we should bring the experience of business leaders to improve the work of the government.

From the discussion with Nilekani, it was clear that there are two different models of how improvement is made in social systems such as cities and large organisations. A popular approach is to first develop a plan, often prepared by experts, which is subsequently rolled out to the organisation by the CEO. Milestones have been fixed, and responsibilities have been established. And an information system is created to enable the CEO to track progress. This top-down change process may often work. But it has a weakness, that the other approach to change that Nilekani explained, does not have. And that weakness is that the top-down process, by definition, requires a strong and committed CEO to drive the change. Therefore when that authority is missing the change slows down, or it may not even start. Hence consultants who prepare detailed blueprints for change say that an essential condition for implementation is a strong CEO to see it through.

The discussion with Nilekani sought to understand his role and that of the Chief Minister in the process of change in Bangalore. The Chief Minister has blessed the process but is apparently not driving it, and Nilekani is not the CEO of Bangalore. So where is the authority that is making the change happen? Nilekani explained where the impetus for change lies. He described the three essential components of the BATF and Janaagraha processes. One is a vision prepared by the heads of the concerned government departments with their short-term plan for the improvements that would be brought about. The second is a platform for them to present their plans to citizens' groups and thereafter periodically report the progress to them. The third component is an information system that enables these officers to track their own budgets and performance and answer the queries of citizens. The Right to Information acts are good moves. But they cannot produce results if officers who want to, do not have the means at their disposal to provide the accurate information.

Notice that both approaches, the conventional top-down approach as well as the middle-out approach used in Bangalore share three essential components: A plan, an accurate information system, and regular reviews. The difference is in the process used. In the top-down approach, an outside expert makes the plan, perhaps with inputs from insiders. In the other approach, responsible insiders make the plans, assisted by facilitators and experts. Another critical difference is the person who monitors progress. In one case, it is the chief, whereas in the other it is the concerned citizens. Therefore, in situations where the boss may change frequently, as often happens within the civil services, or where one strong leader cannot be found, as happens in fluid political situations, the top-down approach cannot work, whereas the other one can. Besides, since the political system in India is not like China's or Singapore's, a model of change in which imposition by authority is essential to produce change may not be appropriate for us.

Another benefit of the Bangalore approach is that the change springs from deeper roots. While initially slower, it is more sustainable because it is founded on commitment from the implementers towards their own aspirational plans rather than compliance with an expert's plans. A CEO's whip and time are not critical requirements for the middle-out approach to work as they are in the top-down approach. For these reasons, several CEOs in the corporate world who have the authority to drive a change through their organisation choose not to do so. Instead, they follow an approach of high involvement and empowerment. Not only is the change deeper and more sustainable but also they are not harried to continuously check and crack the whip. I remember one CEO who proudly showed me the comprehensive and updated information on his computer about the progress of a large change programme. He wanted me to appreciate how much effort he was personally putting into the process. But his complaint was that he was required to chase people all the time. He was working till two in the morning every day and was awake at six again. Why were his people not as committed as he was, he wondered?

Which is the better approach to transformation? Deng Xiao Ping said it doesn't matter whether the cat is black or white so long as it catches the mouse. His point was that the goal is important, and it does not matter how it is reached. Indeed, many roads lead to Rome, as they say. But the only one we can take is the one that starts from where we are. We may want the same results as obtained in Shanghai, but we must discover and use means that fit our democratic conditions. Finally, make no mistake: both approaches require leadership. But the style and means of leadership are different.

7

The
Tower of
Babbling

The problem of his village is still not solved? But we held debates and seminars on the problem. We must hold more seminars and discussions.

7

The Tower of Babbling

The golden rule of conduct is mutual toleration, seeing that we
will never all think alike and we shall always see Truth in
fragments and from different angles of vision

—Mahatma Gandhi

M<small>Y</small> earliest images of the power of India's political leaders
were the mass meetings that they addressed. The images of
thousands of people sitting in the dust; a raised platform with
a cloth canopy, beneath which stood their leader in front of a
microphone, with his (or her, as it was for Indira Gandhi)
entourage seated behind, and conical loudspeakers hung on
bamboo poles amongst the crowd, through which they could
hear their leader's voice.

The people would wait for hours for their leader to show
up. Hawkers roamed among the crowds selling snacks. Water
was sometimes provided by the organisers of the rally as a
social service to the masses. I knew where the toilets were—
walls of buildings in the vicinity for the men, and scattered
bushes on the periphery for the women. I could see people
come out searching for relief when I drove by or sometimes

stopped at the edges of the gathering to hear what the leader had to say. Whatever it was, people were willing to listen to it for hours. I could barely see the little figure of the leader in the distance, and the people must have appeared like little insects to him or her. Those were my earliest recollections of leaders and those who were being led, communicating with each other. The leader spoke. The people spoke mostly through their devotion, expressed by their presence, waiting, patient hearing, and their occasional applause. Only later did I learn that the people had been brought to hear the leader; that they had been jammed into buses and trucks; that they may have been promised a snack as an inducement; and that they had no option but to wait long hours in the sun because they could not go back till the trucks and buses were lined up for their return!

When I was the Resident Director of Telco's factory in Pune, Indira Gandhi came to speak at a mass gathering in the city. I was invited by the local Youth Congress chief to hear her. He arranged a seat for me in the front, on a comfortable chair along with other VIPs. We waited and chatted. It was a good time for me to network with others in business and the government. Behind us the masses also waited. I was impressed with Mrs Gandhi's ability to rouse the crowd when she arrived. I could see her clearly when she spoke. She was not speaking to me, however, nor to the people on the chairs. She was speaking to the masses behind us. They applauded from time to time. They were hearing her.

She seemed to have heard them also. Obviously not at such meetings, but somehow, through her party people perhaps, who had time to mingle with the people in their constituencies. The people and she seemed to have connected well with each other because they gave more votes to her and her party than to the alternatives. But the same people also voted her out of power. She had not heard the change in their concerns. Her advisers were blamed for filtering the messages they passed on to her. She had been kept in the dark.

When I moved to the USA, I found that the US Presidents had more sophisticated means to communicate with the people. When I arrived, George Bush senior was the President. There was some concern that he was not in touch with the public, and was not an effective leader. His press secretary countered this impression on a TV show by sharing an internal secret. She said the President looked at the opinion polls every morning and adjusted policies accordingly. On the one hand I was impressed that the President had access to so much unfiltered information directly from the people (or so I thought till I inquired into the process further). On the other hand I had a nagging concern about the President being led by people's opinions rather than having his own convictions that he would not budge from, regardless of popular opinion. Who was leading whom, I wondered? True, the frequent polls gave the US President the means to hear the people at the back of the crowd, that Indian leaders could not achieve in their mass rallies. But what was the US public hearing from their leader? Whereas leaders in India spoke out loudly and long to the gathered masses, what people in the US seemed to be getting from their leader were their own opinions repackaged into attractive sound bites on TV.

I am not a communications expert, and I had hardly come across any in India before I went to the USA. There I found many. These experts were no longer 'hidden persuaders', as McLuhan had described them many years earlier. Now, they were very visible and some were even celebrities. They targeted audiences, chose the best means of reaching them, and told the people what they wanted to hear. It was marketing at its best, using the best technologies available. But with so many millions to hear from, and so many millions to reach, and that too through brief communications to suit short attention spans, perhaps there was no alternative to the dumbing down of communication amongst leaders and the masses.

Politics of the people, by the people, was active in New England, where I lived, at the level of towns, and in California at the level of the state where tough propositions were directly put out to vote by the masses. This is how the people decided. It sounded nice, but in practice it could lead to disaster, as it did in California. If people do not have the patience to understand the complexities of inter-related issues, choices have to be simplified for them. Moreover, a straightforward 'aye' or 'nay' voting requires that the choices are made simple. Therefore, voters in California were asked to choose whether or not property taxes should be capped. The answer to that question was: of course, taxes should not increase! Then they were asked whether or not education should remain free. The answer again was: of course, education should remain free! But when the outcomes of such simplistic choices are put together, the system breaks down.

I was one of the massed crowds in the USA. I hardly attended any meetings amongst the leaders of different sections of society—politicians, businessmen, government, and civil society—in which different points of view would be heard and synthesised to develop new policy directions. Nor was I even aware of where and how it happened. Whereas when I came back to India, I was able to participate in such gatherings. And there seemed to be many of them. This seemed to have changed in the decade during which I was away. In the 1980s, businessmen went as supplicants to lobby with government. When the foreign exchange crisis arose in the early 1990s, the erstwhile Finance Minister Manmohan Singh and his team took the industry into confidence. The CII worked with the bureaucrats to develop steps to liberalise the economy, opening the doors to competition for its own members. The spirit in which CII worked, putting the interests of the country ahead of the sections of its own membership earned it respect from the government and society. Ministers and secretaries of government were now willing to participate in public discussions organised by the CII.

When I returned in 2000, I was struck by this change from the 1980s. The government policy was openly criticised by businessmen in meetings. Some ministers even appeared to be willing to hear the criticism. Yet something was missing. The country required deeper economic reforms, going beyond the easing of import and industrial licensing regulations, which were the subjects of the first round of reforms by Manmohan Singh and his team. Now public sector enterprises had to be privatised; subsidies for power, gas, and utilities reduced to allow market forces to do their cleansing act in these sectors; and taxes levied by states had to be rationalised to enable integration of the internal Indian market. The stakeholders in these debates went beyond central government ministers, bureaucrats and business leaders. And so the debates were getting stuck between, on one side, demands from business that the centre's coalition government reflect the 'political will' that the Congress Prime Minister Narasimha Rao and Finance Minister Manmohan Singh had earlier demonstrated and, on the other side, pleas from the government that the 'second generation' reforms were politically more complicated than the earlier economic reforms.

What was missing in these debates was the participation of all the stakeholders involved. The central economic establishment of bureaucrats, businessmen, and theoretical economists was talking about the people out there—their hopes and fears; but those people were not in the room. As a result, the discussions became abstract. Business claimed that whatever was good for business had to be good for the people. The government countered that perhaps some large sections of people may not yet think so. Nevertheless, the representatives of those people were never invited to participate in these debates. The speakers at the conventions were always drawn from the same

establishment, with international business leaders and economists invited to add colour. However, these international speakers
were even more remote from the reality of the people of
India and their advice to the Indian government to strengthen
its spine and get on with it, sounded even further removed
from reality.

When I first suggested to the organisers of these conventions
that the representatives of other constituencies should be invited
to speak, I was told that business executives would not come
to a convention to listen to such people. The delegates at these
conventions wanted to hear from important leaders from business
and government and it would be a waste of their time to hear
other, 'unimportant' speakers. In a few months, however, I
began to hear frustration with the content and format of the
conventions. The content was limited as a result of excluding
voices that needed to be heard for the systemic problems to be
understood. And the format did not even allow the narrow
set of stakeholders who were invited to express themselves.
The important dignitaries on the dais gave speeches. If there
was any time, a few questions from the floor were answered
perfunctorily. It was not quite as bad as the mass rallies
with thousands of people sitting in the dust and the speakers
lecturing to them from their high platforms. But the
communication was essentially a similar, one-way flow from
the dais to the floor.

Soon after my return, a prominent lady who was interested
in improving the quality of education in the country asked me
to help in organising a meeting on the subject. We discussed
the profile of individuals who would be invited to participate
and those who would be asked to speak. She picked a few
names of speakers, and I asked about some others whose views
were known to be radically different. She said it would throw
the meeting into confusion. It was best to play it safe, she
suggested. I asked whether she was interested in having a nice,

superficial meeting or to getting to the heart of the matter. She wanted the latter obviously, she said, but did not know how to do it. I suggested a format to her and offered to manage the meeting. I proposed that we should not have a dais, and that there would be no speeches either. Everyone would get an equal chance to speak if they wanted to. She agreed and she got into the spirit of the meeting wholeheartedly. However, her assistants were not happy with the format. They wanted her to sit on the stage, to make a speech, and be quoted in the media. But she was firm. The participants were surprised with the format. They all got a chance to speak and, more importantly, to listen to the points of view they had no chance to hear, or had shut themselves off from hearing so far. They acknowledged that the insights they got by the dialogue in that meeting were fresh, whereas what they took back from other meetings on education—and they claimed they attended more than one a month—was a repetition of what they already knew, with the same people saying the same things.

Too much information; Very little understanding

'These are times of fast foods but slow digestion', says the Dalai Lama. This describes aptly the state of communications amongst people in the world today. You can never have too much communication in the guidebooks for management of change and resolution of conflict. But you can have communication of the wrong kind. Let us look at some of the common misconceptions about what communication really is.

The first misconception is that communication is about talking to people, and therefore more communication means more talk through speeches, videos, letters, memos, etc. However, talking to people is not enough. They also have to listen. A Zen riddle asks the question, 'Is there a sound in the forest if a tree crashes and there is no one to hear it?' The answer is that there cannot be a sound until the act of hearing it is completed. Similarly, communication cannot be complete until the listener registers the message. Therefore barriers to listening have to be overcome, and repetition of the same message will generally be unable to do this. The filters in the minds of the listeners will block out the message. These filters are the preconceptions in the backs of their heads as we discussed in Chapter 5.

Another misconception is that a presentation of facts can change people's minds. Unfortunately, the mental filters also block out information that does not fit preconceived ideas. Peter Drucker, the management guru, said that he does not ask for the facts first, but asks executives for their opinions first. Because, he says, any executive worth his salt can find facts to support his opinions. Robert McNamara, a brilliant executive, was CEO of the Ford Motor Company, and later the Secretary of Defense under both President Kennedy and President Johnson. He reflects on the lessons of his life, in the documentary 'The Fog of War'. The grand theme that runs through this documentary is the human capacity for self-deception, and the way that our perceptions are shaped by our beliefs. Some incidents that were reported to have taken place in the Vietnam War were fictitious, and numbers were distorted. Errol Morris, the producer of the documentary comments, 'The mind is very accommodating. It fills in the blanks for you, even when there are no blanks to be filled in.'

The third misconception is that access to a breadth of information broadens people's minds. There has been a veritable explosion in the amount of information and variety of opinions that people in economically advanced nations can access in the media and on the Internet. There is so much information, that people must make choices about what they will pay attention to: which TV shows they will watch, which papers they will read, and which Internet sites they will check. At the same

time, no TV programme, paper, or website can hope to satisfy
everyone, so each targets a select audience, either by the
subjects it concentrates on, or by the slant it gives to the
information it provides. Thus special interest groups
are formed of people who habitually read and see the same
things, which are a small subset of the vast amount of information
they can theoretically access but in practice cannot and will
not do. In the USA, I was struck by, what seemed to me, the
rabid views of well-educated people on issues such as gun
control, abortion, and even evolution. *Time* magazine (December
2003) in an article on the USA, titled 'How we got so divided',
said,

> 'And with the proliferation of the media, Americans do not
> have to listen anymore to people who do not agree with
> them. There's talk radio and cable and Truebeliever.com to
> reinforce and inflame their views rather than challenge
> them. The hordes of media shouters both mirror the electorate
> and harden their outlook. Moderation may be sensible and
> practical, but it's not entertaining, and it doesn't sell books.
> (or TV and radio shows for that matter).'

The disease is not restricted to the USA. It is spreading
everywhere. Another article published in *The Economist* (27
March 2004) analysed the malaise in Germany. It said 'The
media do not help voters grasp that in crisis is opportunity.
News cycles are getting shorter, with trivia leaping into the
headlines and any policy ideas swiftly shredded. Politicians
complain that "tabloidisation" makes it hard to discuss complex
structural reforms. And the press has developed a populist streak.'

The disease has reached India too. It has infected TV, the
print media, and the style of many conventions that often sell
flimsy content packaged into lofty themes. India needs to
worry about this disease of poor communications more than
other countries, because its society is more vulnerable to

fragmentation. Dr Bimal Jalan, wrote in an article titled 'Economics, Politics And Governance' in *The Financial Express* (5 April 2004):

> (Such) special interests are also more diverse (in India) than in other more developed and mature economies. Thus, there are special regional interests, not only amongst states, but also within states. Economic policy-making at the political level is further affected by occupational divide (e.g. farm vs non-farm), the size of the enterprise (e.g. large vs small), caste, religion, political affiliations of trade unions, or asset class of power-wielders.

Better ways to listen and be heard

Good communication perhaps requires more listening than speaking. Talking more loudly will not break through the barriers in communication between people. TV shows like 'Cross Fire' in the USA, and 'The Big Fight' in India in which the participants yell and interrupt each other, are entertaining for their viewers. However, I am sure they do not help the participants understand each other better. The meeting of minds, and change of minds can happen when people really listen to those who have opinions different from their own. When they listen to the others' reasons—why they have their beliefs; and even more, to their emotions—their hopes and fears and when others feel they are being heard, they may be more willing to hear us. Thus we may begin to really communicate with each other.

Enormous amounts of time, effort, and money are being expended in people talking at each other in conventions and being bombarded with information through a variety of media. But the amount of high fidelity communication as a result of such conversations is meagre. We have to find better ways of communicating that enable deeper listening, and thereby improve communion amongst people. Such ways are available. Their heritage is in the art of dialogue and traditions of group meetings such as the Quakers', rather than in advertising and mass communications whose concepts and techniques increasingly drive the design of communications in media and conventions. Good facilitators enable people to listen to their own unarticulated beliefs and aspirations and to each other.

One problem with these alternative approaches is that they require much more time than people feel they can spare from their busy, chattering lives. They generally seem to require people to shut off their daily routines and meet 'off-site' for days. Another limitation is that only a few people at a time can participate in the meetings. However the gains can be enormous. Borrowing poet Rabindranath Tagore's immortal words, these alternative formats of communion can enable clear streams of reason to emerge from the dreary desert sand of dead habit, and they can breach the narrow domestic walls that are breaking the world into fragments.

These approaches are evolving in response to the need within society for more effective communication. The Aspen Institute in the USA uses such approaches. The Society of Organisational Learning with headquarters in MIT in the USA has grown into an international network that is researching better methods. The International Futures Forum based in St Andrews, Scotland, is another incubator. And there are others in many parts of the world.

My hope is that India will be at the centre of this evolution. India is its best laboratory and has the greatest need for it. No other country in the world has the diversity within it as is present in India. Eighteen distinct languages with myriad dialects; all the major religions in the world; and wide disparities in incomes. This diversity of people has chosen to work together democratically, which implies listening to the needs and wants of all. The people have an enormous task to accomplish together in order to change and improve their country, to make it fully developed, which is an expression of their vision for the country. What the people want, and what they believe in, needs to be understood amongst them. And what they do, has to be aligned towards their shared vision to accelerate sustainable change.

India needs simple techniques for communication amongst diverse people to facilitate the collaboration in townships and in villages to make the new India come about. Such techniques may do for India what TQM techniques did for Japan. Japan picked itself up from a shattering defeat in the Second World War and became an industrial power—the 'machine that changed the world'. A principal contribution to Japan's success were the seven tools of quality control developed by Dr Ishikawa and others. These were widely disseminated by JUSE (the Japanese Union of Scientists and Engineers) through public radio, books, pamphlets, seminars, and schools. These tools provided a simple and powerful language for workmen on shop floors, offices, construction sites, and elsewhere to work together to improve quality. The beauty of these tools was that they enabled everyone to take responsibility for quality by applying them to the work that they performed every day. These tools have since been adopted throughout the world and have contributed enormously to the improvement of economic efficiency. Perhaps some simple techniques for effective listening and communication should be developed in India soon so that it can become the way in which Indians everywhere improve the manner in which they work and create together. These techniques, founded on the same principles that enable great communication to take place in the intense off-sites that I referred to earlier, will make these principles practically applicable in daily life, just as the seven tools of quality took quality from the experts' labs to factories and offices in Japan.

Experience suggests that such techniques, founded on good principles of communication, if diligently practised, could work wonders in India. I have been able to slip these principles and techniques into many meetings where people from different walks of life have gathered, such as the Leadership Conclave organised by CII in Goa in December 2003, and the more extensive 'generative scenario thinking' process sponsored by CII in 1999. The participants in such meetings always comment on the profound difference they perceive in the tone and quality of communication amongst them and the fresh insights they obtain.

Entertainment sans
Edification

*The media and organisers of seminars have become too focussed
on selling their wares. Hence the quality of information
available to the public and the depth of public discourse has
deteriorated dangerously*

'WE live in a time of fast foods but slow digestion', said
His Holiness the Dalai Lama. Two stories published in *The
Times of India* reminded me of these wise words. One was a
story of the arrival of the World Wrestling Federation (WWF)
in India. It said the wrestlers with outlandish names were
'rehearsing' for the big fights that would be staged in a few
days. Evidently they were checking out the sound effects of
their grunts and the choreography of their throws. Clearly the
WWF is not about sports. It is entertainment; and people are
willing to pay a lot of money for it. The other story, about
management guru Tom Peters' seminar, said many people had
paid as much as Rs 25,000 each to hear Peters entertain them

Article first published in *The Economic Times*.

with his irreverent pot shots at the corporate world. The story went on to say that Peters did not say anything profound but the audience enjoyed itself thoroughly. I fear that in India we are sliding inexorably into an age of more information and less wisdom, and much entertainment with less content—a path the USA has gone down already.

One of the first pieces of advice given to me by my American colleagues in the consulting firm I joined in the USA in 1989 was to make sure that I grabbed the attention of senior executives in the first five minutes. 'If they don't get it in five minutes, you have lost them. The attention span of CEOs is very short,' I was told. Some years later I wrote a book, *The Accelerating Organisation*, and on the advice of my publisher in New York, I made it very accessible for senior executives—a euphemism for making it simple, with short lists of things to do. I asked my friend, Peter Senge, author of *The Fifth Discipline*, to review the manuscript and consider writing a preface. He gave a warm endorsement to the ideas in the book. But he said he would not write the preface because he could not endorse the easy style of the book! 'The problem is that US executives have become intellectually lazy,' he said, 'Spoiled by consultants like you who want to sell them ready-made food in easy to chew morsels. Therefore, they are losing the ability for serious reflection. And the world will not change until CEOs seriously apply their own minds to difficult issues!'

Senge's *The Fifth Discipline* became a bestseller when it was published 10 years back. However, most people who bought the book did not read it. They found it to be heavy reading. Senge delighted in his book's reputation—the least read management bestseller ever! These can be contrasted with another, much more successful bestseller—Blanchard's *One Minute Manager*. Even its title makes Senge's point. I have written earlier about the shallowness of debates on TV that are designed for entertainment rather than edification: Shows like 'The Big Fight' and 'Crossfire'. They have values akin to those of WWF shows. But they manage to sell. And that is what matters at the end of the day in this age of commercialisation.

In August this year, the Aspen Institute organised a serious seminar at Aspen, on 'Global Capitalism and Development', in which the participants had to do the work. Neither were there snazzy presentations nor speeches to sit back and listen to. The participants had to read, share their views, listen to others, and synthesise ideas. It was a great learning experience for the 20 senior executives who attended the seminar. Jerry Levin, who had just retired as the CEO of AOL TimeWarner, the global media giant, led a discussion on the role of the media. The US media is increasingly becoming a brew of technology, journalism, and entertainment, illustrated by the combination of AOL, Time-Life and Warner Brothers. And with the global spread of capitalism, US media formats are pervading other cultures. It is not only the content of the global news and views that the US media can influence, it is also the style, and arguably, the shallowness of the discourse in the mass media. Participants at the seminar from Europe and Asia expressed their concern with this situation.

The question then was who has the responsibility to change this trend: The US media that is producing the stuff, or the societies that do not want their citizens to consume it? If people want it, what is wrong in supplying it, was the US view? The riposte was, why does the US government go after those who produce drugs in Colombia and other countries? If US citizens want to buy cocaine, what is wrong with poor farmers in Colombia producing it for them? If our minds are indeed becoming lazy, the issue is who is responsible for reversing the trend. Perhaps it is a shared responsibility between the consumer and the provider who are symbiotically linked. But someone has to initiate the discussion for the need for change. Who shall lead it?

The 'WMD' We Really Want

The WMD we really need to find and develop now are 'Ways of Mass Dialogue'; without them we risk tearing the world apart, environmentally, politically, and socially

W E live in a world that is struggling to be one, and in a country that has chosen to combine many disparate people into one nation. However, national interests and communal differences break us apart. Further, our knowledge is broken into many scientific disciplines. When we turn to our scientists and experts for solutions, we get a babble of scientific and pseudo-scientific languages. This is an unintended consequence of the very desirable development of scientific disciplines with the Enlightenment that spread across the world since the eighteenth century. What we need now is a second Enlightenment to integrate insights from the lenses of many disciplines to understand the whole, not merely the parts, and see the linkages thereafter.

Article first published in *The Economic Times*.

For a 100 years and more, scientists have been vigorously pursuing insights into the infinitely small building blocks of our world, such as subatomic particles and genes. And now little things, running out of control, threaten to destroy the world, like the power within nuclei and germs. Hence the campaign by the large nations that made these discoveries to prevent such potent weapons of mass destruction (WMD) from falling into the hands of tiny bands of terrorists. If I was on the governing board of World Inc. and had to recommend the portfolio of research projects to make the world a better place in the twenty-first century, I would strongly recommend that we devote more of our best minds, time and money to develop another class of WMD—Ways of Mass Dialogue—rather than more research into the physical world. Because recent events clearly show that it is our inability to listen to each other and to have effective dialogues that is weakening the very institutions we need to govern, shape and create a better world.

Let me begin with the relatively small issues and then go on to the very large—from breakdowns in corporate governance to the crumbling of the international order. There was a flurry of reaction in the USA and elsewhere to several embarrassing failures in corporate governance. Committees were set up and several new legislations were introduced. However consensus has emerged that new rules and structures may have little effect. What is really required is an improvement in the quality of discussions in board meetings to enable independent voices to be heard and entrenched positions to be challenged.

Nations are much more complex than corporations. Many stakeholders have to work together to develop the economy and society, even as they compete with each other. Political parties, business corporations and civil organisations, collaborating and clashing, are all part of this swirling stew. The greater the diversity of people, as there is in India, the greater is the need to understand different perspectives. Moreover, the stronger the regard for democracy and the rights of people to have a say, the more complicated is the process of alignment. And the greater the urgency for faster development, as in India, the larger the frustration with the inability of the whole to get together and move on. These three Ds put together—diversity, democracy, and development—make political leadership a special challenge. It would be far easier if one of the three were taken out. But which one? Clearly we cannot afford to let go of any of them. Therefore the simplistic calls for increased 'political will', with which many of our discussions about India's development end, are naive. The solution lies elsewhere: In a fourth D—which is effective public dialogue to align multifarious interests.

Something serious ails the world as well. Terrorism and poverty are scourges that are disturbing the lives and consciences of people everywhere. Can solutions to these global problems lie merely in the realm of economists and in the institutions of global trade and finance such as the WTO and IMF? How shall we address concerns about sovereign rights of countries and accountability of elected governments to their constituents? And what about concerns for the environment, human rights, and other issues that NGOs want to address? At the global level also we have a messy tangling of economics and politics with an increasingly concerned civil society. Therefore the need for effective dialogue is very palpable in the international arena. Many bilateral and multilateral trade and political issues are bogged down by hardening positions. In all of them there is frustration at the very least; some have spilled into violence; and in a few there is even fear that someone or the other may be tempted to use the wrong WMD—those tiny destructive things that unfortunately get into the hands of terrorists and governments. Why cannot we get together and talk through the issues instead? Is it because we do not want to, or because we do not know how to have an effective dialogue? I will presume the ultimate good intent even in those who step out of the discussion. I believe they are frustrated with the messy process of discussion. But their withdrawal makes it impossible for the process to succeed. This results in a potentially deadly downward spiral. Therefore it is imperative that we improve the quality of the dialogue in the first place.

Through the ages, the method of adversarial debate has been used in Western cultures to explore issues, whether in lawcourts, political assemblies, or academic institutions. Western methods of inquiry are rooted deeply in the methods of the Greeks, of Aristotle and Socrates. Aristotle regarded logic as the only trustworthy means for human judgement. Emotions, he said, get in the way. Furthermore, Aristotelian philosophy, with its emphasis on formal logic, was based on the assumption that truth is gained by opposition. We have interpreted the type of argumentation that Socrates favoured, the Socratic method, as systematically leading an opponent to admitting error, and primarily a way of showing up an adversary as having been in the wrong. We parry individual points brought up by our opponents, and rarely step back to actively imagine a world in which a different system of ideas could be true.

A big problem with this approach of inquiring into issues is that when one side has been shown to have lost, and perhaps been insulted in the bargain, it becomes very difficult to arrive at a consensus between the adversaries thereafter. The Navajo Indians believe that if one ends a dispute by having a winner and a loser, one dispute may have ended but another will surely have started, because harmony will not have been restored.

Another serious limitation of adversarial debates is that issues have to be broken out into two sides: one for and one against. There is no provision in this black and white world for examining issues that have three or more sides or points of view as most complex issues may have. If we all have to share one world and if we really believe in respecting the rights of every human being to life, dignity, and a fair chance in this world, then we must consider what all people need and want. Can we presume to speak for others, especially those who seem very different from us in the way they think? Shall we debate them to decide who is right and who is wrong, or subjugate their ideas in other ways if debates with them are tiresome? We must now engage in dialogues to learn, not in debates to win.

Dialogue is a mode of deep conversation that must be distinguished from two other, more usual modes of conversation. These others, as described by Otto Scharmer of MIT, are debate and downloading. In downloading, by far the most common form, we say what we are expected to say and what we already know. This is the mode used at social gatherings and most conferences. The conversation stays on the surface. Nothing new emerges. No wonder these meetings are so unproductive. Debating, which is common in organisations with an intellectual bent, involves dissecting problems with facts. In debates, we dig deeper but positions can become more entrenched. Generally nothing new is created again. Dialogue, on the other hand, calls on us to be empathetic—to see the world through the eyes of others—and self-reflective—to understand how we influence the world around us. In dialogue I listen and open myself to change because I genuinely wish to learn. Whereas in a debate I want to prove my point and win the argument. The competitive spirit of debates is entertaining no doubt, and hence the mass media take advantage of it in popular shows like 'The Big Fight,' 'Cross Fire', and 'Face Off'. This is the mode of discussion that the world is getting used to, unfortunately.

The art of dialogue has been around since pre-modern times in many parts of the world. For instance, tribes of American Indians (living not far from Los Alamos where the atomic bomb was later developed) had mastered skills of deep listening. The challenge of the twenty-first century is to find ways to make dialogue not only deeper but also broader and faster. The world has become highly interconnected. It cannot any longer be 'broken up into fragments by narrow domestic walls' (as Tagore once said). Speed is essential too. Many time bombs are ticking all over the world. Therefore, the development and use of effective Ways of Mass Dialogue should be the highest priority for the world. A group of international practitioners, with experience in other countries, have proposed a 'global dialogue lab'. I would urge India to be at the forefront of the development and use such new WMD because we desperately need this technology for our progress.

In India, we need faster economic growth to provide gainful employment to millions of young people and defuse a possible political explosion. At the same time, to create conditions for economic growth, we have to stop people from expressing their frustrations in destructive ways. We may be close to entering a vicious spiral in which the breakdown of cooperation will slow economic growth, leading to more frustration, and thus more disorder. To stop us from slipping in, we urgently need dialogues between people divided by history and between experts divided by disciplines.

What should the dialogue be about? The first dialogue must be about the alternative means we will use to resolve differences—alternatives to violence, and supplements to the official, political and parliamentary processes. Violence is unacceptable. The official processes are not working.

Where will this dialogue take place? It cannot take place within the official parliamentary system. It must be an 'unofficial' process so that it is not trapped within the limitations of the official system that it is supposed to supplement. Joseph Nye, the former dean of the Kennedy School of Government, commenting on global governance in *Parliament of Dreams*, said, 'The prospects of an institution of global governance are slim, given our underdeveloped sense of democracy.' In India, let us admit that while we may be proud of our democracy—which happens to be the world's largest, unfortunately, it remains underdeveloped.

How will the dialogue be different from the debates that are taking place? First, a dialogue is certainly not a physical process with scuffles and frequent walkouts, which is what our parliamentary process often degenerates into. Second, it is not a debate in which people are compelled to advocate opposing points of view, but a process during which people rise above their different perspectives. Third, a dialogue is not a summation of many monologues, which is what most of our seminars turn out to be. A dialogue requires participative formats that facilitate listening, inquiry, and exploration, not speeches from a panel with perfunctory questions and answers. We urgently need effective dialogues to help stop the bleeding of our national potential and the lives of our people.

Who will sponsor this process? In South Africa, when the country was being torn apart with racial differences and violence in the early 1990s, businessmen took the lead. They invited a group of people from politics, academia, and business to get together outside the official processes of negotiations for a dialogue on South Africa's future. The scenarios and insights they produced helped lubricate the official processes of negotiation that resulted in the end of apartheid. Maybe we need to start this process in India as well?

8

Shaping India

... our dreams can be realized if the people unite and cooperate ...'
or is it 'the ministers unite and cooperate', sir?

8

Shaping India

Each of us must be the change we want to see in the world

—Mahatma Gandhi

I began this book by noting concerns from several quarters in India and abroad about the way in which India is headed. I recounted critical turning points in my own life that led me to explore how organisations and societies learn and change. Thereafter I presented the Learning Field, a framework for organisational learning and change. In the following four chapters, I explained the power of the concepts in this framework and their relevance to India through a combination of stories and articles.

In this last chapter I look forward to the future of India. The future cannot be as precisely described as the past. So the style of the word-painting will change. It will be in broader brush-strokes, with less detail, leaving more to the imagination of the reader. The painting is an ideogram—a word picture—with five broad, intersecting strokes. Each of these strokes has been rehearsed before and is a piece from other documents that I have written. These documents, written separately, described different facets of India. As the reader may see, they intersect and evoke rich possibilities for India's future.

The first stroke, *Resources For The Future,* takes a broad sweep at the history of global economic development. It suggests that a confluence of mega forces is providing India a unique opportunity that no nation has had before.

The second, sharp stroke, *A High Leverage Initiative to Accelerate Change,* looks beneath the surface at currents within India, and points to the critical leverage point to make change happen.

The third stroke, *An Invitation to Make a Difference,* takes up from the second and suggests the way in which such a change can be brought about.

The fourth stroke, *Planning for Commitment, Not Compliance,* confirms the suggestion with an analysis of why the prevalent ways have not worked well.

And the fifth, *Fireflies Arising,* is a sweep of colour to bring the picture to life.

The five bold, broad strokes together evoke a picture of how the people of India can shape their future. The paint used for these brushstrokes will seem familiar to the reader, because it is composed of ideas that have already been discussed in the book.

1. Resources for the future

(From the Report of the High Level Strategic Group in 2003, titled *India's New Opportunity 2020: 40 Million New Jobs; $200 Billion Additional Revenue)*

The steam engine (and its successor, the internal combustion engine) heralded the industrial revolution that led to economic growth in the West. These engines required fuel—coal and petroleum. As the industrialised countries exhausted their own sources of supply they turned increasingly to other sources, which resulted in the economic growth of the supplying countries, such as the oil producing countries of the Middle East. This pattern is unfolding again. The growth paradigm of Western economies requires another kind of fuel—knowledge workers and skilled professionals. For example, US growth rates of the 1990s are primarily attributed to productivity increases enabled by a highly skilled workforce. In the next two decades developed countries will face a shortfall of fuel (skilled professionals) and once again will have to look towards developing countries to make up for the shortfall.

For India, growth is an imperative necessity. To be counted as a major economic powerhouse by the end of this century's first quarter, India needs to accelerate its economic growth beyond the existing rates of 5–6 per cent per annum. Then only can its citizens, more than a quarter of whom (about 28 per cent) currently live below the poverty line, afford better lifestyles. In addition, at current growth rates India is projected to have a significant unemployed population (estimates range from 19 to 37 million unemployed by 2012), the largest share of which would be educated youth. The unemployment and poverty resulting from inadequate growth will retard other efforts to place India amongst the top global economic powers. Therefore, the acceleration of economic growth and the employment of skilled youth in the next two decades are key concerns for India Inc.

Perhaps we have for too long looked to others for models of growth. We have marvelled at the tigers and the dragon and wondered what we could do to copy their success. But that is denying ourselves our unique place in the world. Perhaps if we start with our own strengths, we can find an opportunity in our uniquely large and skilled workforce—an opportunity that distinguishes our model of growth that is opening up for India as a result of global developments this report analyses. While India faces an unemployment crisis, ironically, many countries are projected to face workforce shortages in the same period due to lower birth rates and an increase in the proportion of the elderly in their population. While skilled workforce requirements are increasing in line with economic growth, availability is not keeping pace, as a result of fewer people entering the workforce and the trend towards early retirement. Select professions are already witnessing a shortfall (IT services, medical, education). The workforce shortages (mostly in skilled categories) can slow down economic growth in these countries and have other adverse socio-economic implications. Adjusting for initiatives taken by governments to manage this crisis, the High Level Strategic Group (HLSG) estimates a net workforce shortfall of 32–39 million by 2020 in the developed countries of today.

This challenge faced by some countries presents a great opportunity for some developing countries, such as India. India can target this shortage by providing remote services to these countries and also by importing customers and servicing their needs in India. The contribution of remote services alone, which is the main focus of this report, will be $133–315 billion of additional revenue flowing into the country and the addition of 10–24 million jobs (direct and indirect) by 2020. Further, importing customers into India (medical tourism, educational services, leisure tourism) could add $6–50 billion in revenue and create 10–48 million jobs (direct and indirect) by 2020. HLSG estimates that through remote services and the importation of customers India could enhance year-to-year GDP growth by up to 1.5 per cent over current growth rates, most of which (80–85 per cent) would be through remote services.

India is positioned well against these opportunities, given its large pool of qualified manpower, track record in service delivery in sectors like IT, and lower costs of service (specifically in areas such as medical treatment and education services). However, in order to convert these opportunities into actual revenues, India Inc. will have to take several initiatives.

The HLSG has identified six thrust areas for action to boost the demand for India's services:

- ❏ Strengthen India Inc. image/brand.
- ❏ Focus marketing on select countries with select services.
- ❏ Build customer credibility.
- ❏ Promote acceptability of the 'offshore' concept.
- ❏ Improve service experience for customers.
- ❏ Invest in promoting trials.

HLSG has also identified six thrust areas for action to boost the supply of India's services:

- ❏ Develop domain expertise in specific areas.
- ❏ Reform education and the training sector to increase the base of skilled professionals.
- ❏ Strengthen connectivity infrastructure (telecom, IT, airports).
- ❏ Promote public–private partnerships.
- ❏ Form interest groups around opportunities.
- ❏ Align legal and regulatory structure.

2. A high leverage initiative to accelerate change

(This is the substance of a note I wrote in 1998 to two friends who were in senior positions with the Indian government, both of whom were interested to explore alternative approaches to central planning to accelerate the development of India. They both supported a pilot to try some of the tools proposed. The pilot, using the techniques of 'generative scenario thinking' validated the efficacy of the approach proposed. The story of that pilot was written in my earlier book, *Shaping The Future: Aspirational Leadership in India and Beyond*, published by John Wiley and Sons)

The Indian social-political-economic system appears unable to accelerate improvement of the whole system. This is leading to frustrations within the system. Some are expressing this frustration in unilateral, self-serving, and often violent behaviour. Others are opting out of the system. Many others are becoming increasingly passive. All of these behaviours are draining the positive energy from the system at a time when more alignment and constructive action is required.

'Rational' people in the system, who are concerned with the good of the whole, continue to express their concerns and to discuss the situation in an intellectual mode. These discussions take place in meetings of many forums in many settings at which information, warnings, advice, examples, and solutions are offered. These meetings often also include people from outside the Indian system who are invited to give advice, examples, and solutions.

These intellectual discussions help, but do not go very far towards addressing the fundamental inability of the system to take purposeful action. Conveners of these forums try harder by inviting even more illustrious speakers and by increasing the size of the forums. There is a flickering hope, but at the end of the day no significant, if any, improvement is visible in the ability of the system to act. This further builds up frustration (Figure 8.1).

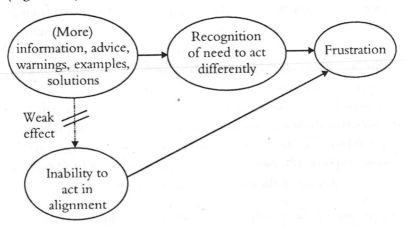

Figure 8.1: Frustration Builds Up

Meanwhile, some actors in the system, frustrated by the lack of progress, and others taking advantage of the inability of the whole to act collectively, 'take the law into their own hands'. They disrupt the system in various ways, sometimes violently, further weakening the system's ability to act, which leads to increase in frustration, thereby setting in motion a vicious downward spiral (Figure 8.2).

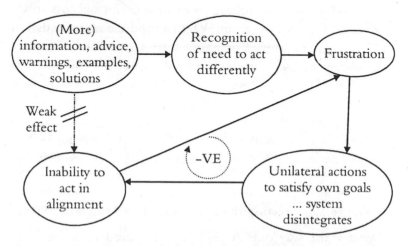

Figure 8.2: System Begins to Disintegrate

Feelings of helplessness to arrest this downward spiral lead some people to suggest that we may need an authoritarian central power, or a 'benevolent dictator', to make things happen. Such thoughts of giving up our independence and democratic values are expressions of extreme helplessness in getting our own act together. If we act on these thoughts, we may address some of the symptoms of our underlying problems, but we will only postpone addressing the root cause of the problem which is our inability to act interdependently in ways that will improve the whole of which each of us is a part. The whole, of course, is the social-political-economic system of India (Figure 8.3).

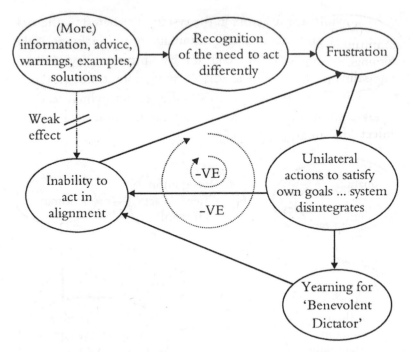

Figure 8.3: Treating the Symptoms in a Dangerous Way

What is the way out? A process is required to address the root cause itself: That is the inability of the system to act purposefully in ways that will benefit the whole (Figure 8.4).

On one hand, actors in the system must also be free to act in their own self-interest. After all, 'rational self-interest' is an underlying premise of modern economic thought, and respect for individuals is a value that is upheld in democratic societies. The 'self-interest' of these actors would also extend to the interests of the institutions they are responsible for. But, on the other hand, the 'self-interested' actions of these actors should, at the very least, be neutral with respect to the performance of the whole. Preferably, their actions should enhance the condition and performance of the whole. Because the bigger and better the pie, the greater the value of their individual slices of it. Appropriate techniques and tools are required for this enabling process of obtaining alignment.

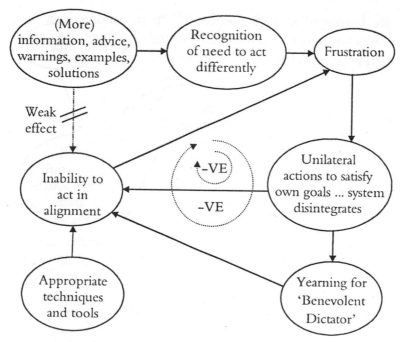

Figure 8.4: Getting at the Root Cause

We are now operating in an open system in which the various parts are connected fluidly with each other, both within our Indian system as well as with the extended world outside India. Such complex, open systems cannot be completed mapped, programmed, or controlled. But they can be understood.

Traditional planning and management techniques have concentrated on the need for prediction and control. They apply well to closed systems. (Hence when the system goes out of control, a rational instinct is to close down the connections of the system with other systems over which the decision-makers do not have control by imposing restrictions or, in the extreme, isolating the system.)

However, new techniques and tools are now available for aiding the process of thinking for open systems. The relevant techniques for the broad policy-making arena are scenario thinking and systems thinking (Figure 8.5). These techniques have been applied with positive effects to national scenarios, such as South Africa, Japan, and Colombia, as well as to interdisciplinary problems such as environmental management.

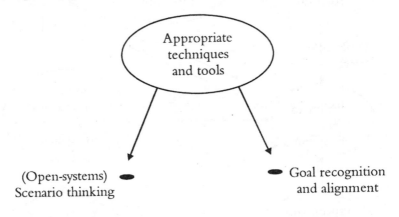

Figure 8.5: A Process for Working in Open Systems with Emotional Actors

Traditional planning techniques are also limited in their ability to factor in and manage the emotional needs of the principal actors in the system. In their drive for rationality and quantification, they either totally ignore or inadequately address the very real and powerful emotional motivations of people. Techniques and tools for vision alignment enable groups of interacting players to include such 'softer' factors in the planning process in a very deliberate and purposeful manner. These techniques are based on the principles of organisational learning.

Finally, it is necessary to state that there is no guarantee that this process will work. But, the question is, 'If not this, then what?' A follow-on question is, 'What do we lose by trying, when there is much to hope for and gain?' (Figure 8.6).

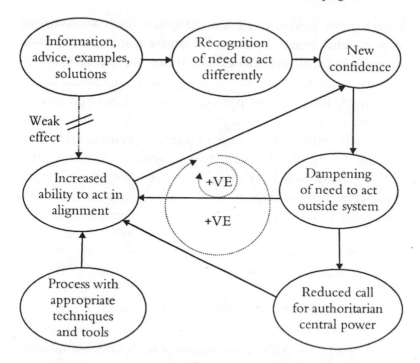

Figure 8.6: Addressing the Root Cause can Generate a Positive Cycle of Change.

3. An invitation to make a difference

(Extract from *Scenarios for India 2010: Putting it Together Again* prepared by CII and The Boston Consulting Group in 2000 to report the outcome of the pilot process of 'generative scenario thinking' in India)

The problem

Many thinking and caring people in our country are concerned about where the country is headed. There is frustration with the slow progress in the country's economic growth, and on the situation of the lot of the poor people of our country.

Many experts, Indian as well as foreign, have proposed solutions to accelerate change. There is no doubt that there has been progress. But it is insufficient and it is slow. Fifty years after our Independence, we have 36 per cent of our population below the poverty line,[1] and 44 per cent of our adult population is illiterate. And many countries that were poorer than us are now much further ahead. On the Human Development Index,[2] we rank 128 among 174 countries, behind Sri Lanka, China, Mexico, and South Africa. Similarly, on the Growth Competitiveness Index,[3] we rank 49th among 59 countries, once again behind the above-mentioned countries.

We are a large country, with a lot of diversity. There are so many divisions within the country: many political parties, regions, religions, economic strata, etc. We are very proud of the fact that we are the world's largest democracy. The democratic process requires that different interests must be considered. However, the way the process is playing out in India is getting messier with various groups acting blatantly in their self-interest. The parliamentary process, by which the many interests have to be finally reconciled, now seems to be anything but a good and reasonable process in our country. Often it is chaotic.

The acceleration of change in the country will require aligned action by many groups across the country: civil society, government, business, and political parties. Our problem is that when we go one step forward we invariably have to go half a step backward because of protests from those who are

---

[1] Source: India Economic Survey 1999-2000

[2] The Human Development Index measures average achievement in basic human development in one simple composite index. It is based on 3 indicators—longevity, educational attainment, and standard of living.

[3] The Growth Competitiveness Index measures the factors that contribute to future growth of an economy, in order to explain why some countries attain prosperity faster than others.

adversely affected. Hence the continuing concern amongst investors: Will India carry on with its process of reforms swiftly?

There are already many forums for discussion and debate amongst the many groups who must be consulted. These include the parliamentary process, as mentioned earlier. There are also numerous formal and informal meetings outside the parliamentary process, such as meetings sponsored by industry associations between business people and the government. Nevertheless, the alignment and action is insufficient. And hence there is frustration.

Solving India's endemic problems

Many complex, systemic, problems have to be solved to accelerate the desired change in India. The inadequacy of the education system is one. The poor quality of the physical infrastructure is another. The chronic, and deteriorating power and water supply is yet another issue. All such complex problems require many people from different institutions and with different perspectives to work together. However, they are not working together effectively, which is why these problems have become endemic in nature.

Fortunately, many people have now begun to come forward to address parts of these complex problems, realising that the government alone cannot solve them. These include corporations, NGOs, individuals, as well as motivated government officials. This is a welcome development but can lead to complications that need to be managed.

The complications could arise from two sources. One is the incomplete understanding amongst those who want to generate positive change, about the nature of the whole system and the interactions of the various forces within it. The other is the egos of the various people who need to interact in order to solve problems. In the story of the four blind men and the elephant, each sees the whole in terms of the part he knows best. The knowledge of all the four has to be combined to understand the whole. And they need to do this before they rush into action based on their narrow perceptions, to avoid causing damage or hurt. What if the man who thought the trunk was a tree, took an axe to chop it, or climb it? For example, consider the problem of inadequate and poor education at the school level. It cannot be solved merely by changing the content of the education, nor by merely providing computers to schools. The whole must be understood by combining the knowledge of the experts of the various parts. Only then can their actions contribute to an effective solution to the problem affecting them, and many others.

A fresh national conversation

We need a supplemental process in which various groups can come together with a different spirit. For this to be possible, we recommend a process that has been found to be very powerful in creating deep conversations and learning amongst people who are a part of one large system, but who also compete amongst themselves and perhaps have different values. And who can, by acting in their own self-interest, inadvertently damage the whole of which they are a part.

The process is 'generative scenario thinking.' It has been used with positive effects in many complicated situations. For example, it was used in the early 1990s in South Africa when the differences between the various races and political parties could have blown the country apart.

Indians who care to make a difference need a different approach to thinking and working on today's problems. If many caring Indians act together, putting their weight behind the drivers that can really change the country, we will get the India we want. As Robert Kennedy said in a speech in South Africa:

It is from numberless diverse acts of courage and belief that the human story is shaped. Each time a man stands up for an idea or acts to improve the lot of others or strikes out against injustice, he sends forth a tiny ripple of hope. And crossing each other from a million different centers of energy and daring those ripples build a current that can sweep the mightiest walls of oppression and resistance.

What will you do to make a difference?

4. Planning for commitment, not compliance

(Extract from the High Level Strategic Group's report in 2003 on *India's New Opportunity 2020*)

A key consideration for the HLSG during the development of this report was its ability to bring about real change. To this end, the HLSG invested significant time in understanding the reasons why India, despite having sufficient knowledge of what needs to be done, often fails to 'make it happen.' The collective experience of the HLSG members suggested that the inability to make things happen faster, with alignment, is the main reason behind why India misses opportunities. On further study, it was felt that the lack of speed was generally a result of an implementation model that enforces compliance rather than obtaining commitment. The power of commitment amongst stakeholders to relentlessly obtain the desired outcome cannot be underestimated. Unfortunately, most approaches to implement change are designed to obtain compliance rather than commitment. As a result, the energy in the process peters out. To obtain commitment from all stakeholders, the HLSG embarked on a path that architects and guides the process of involvement and action using the report as a stimulus.

Over the last few years, many reports have been written on how to lead India onto the path of accelerated development.

While most reports correctly identify opportunities and build a coherent roadmap, they often do not result in effective implementation and hence opportunities are not realised. We would like our report to stimulate actions towards the goal. Therefore, we have analysed why reports fail to engage the implementers, and we have used this understanding to shape our report. We have found that reports that fail to have much impact fall into two categories:

- The first category involves a lot of analysis and lays down detailed sets of instructions for those who have to implement whatever ideas are in the report. The focus of the process is to first complete the report. Once completed, such reports often end up on the shelf. The biggest shortcoming in such cases is that the people who have to implement the instructions do not fully comprehend what needs to be done and/or do not take ownership of the task, as they are not involved in its development process.
- The second category starts by analysing the situation and outlining broad themes. However, the follow-up process is not documented well and is largely unstructured. The driving principle in this case is to provide an idea and hope that it will work. Here again, the report hits the shelf and gathers dust.

This report takes a different approach. The approach adopted here rests on two simple principles, which have been found to be highly effective in situations involving disparate interest groups:

1. Create an appreciation of the opportunities that exist and prioritise areas for action.
2. Align processes and participants (implementation partners) towards a common goal.

The chosen approach was based on the analysis of several initiatives, some of them national in scope, and some within corporations. In almost all cases, the members reached a similar conclusion—the quality of process has a far greater impact on the outcome than the amount of detail (recommendations) in the report.

5. Fireflies arising

(This is a brief description of the preferred scenario developed for India by the process of generative scenario thinking'. It was published in the report *Scenarios for India 2010: Putting it Together Again*)

The country has been transformed. All over the country, communities have taken charge of themselves. With assistance from government and NGOs, villages have harvested water. Sanitation has been improved.

Innovations in telecommunication infrastructure by many Indian entrepreneurs have provided almost every village with access to the Internet. Farmers track the prices of their produce, and also the availability of seeds and fertilisers to find the best times and markets to buy and sell. They bank via the Internet. As do many small enterprises in villages.

Many business leaders from the cities have discovered the reliability of women, related perhaps to their sense of responsibility for their children and families. They have put women at the centre of innovative approaches to engage local communities with new business opportunities. Now women play a very large role in the new rural economy. This has brought them into contact with new ideas.

Innovations in the delivery of education have enabled children and adults to acquire knowledge and skills relevant to their needs. The Internet has contributed to this. This has been supplemented by schemes to use the time of retired people and part-timers. Besides, creative use of space available in the communities has reduced the expenditure required to build new schools. Education is accelerating real improvement in the conditions of the poorer parts of the country. And people are making much of the improvement themselves.

Enlightened corporations have been an important catalyst for accelerating these changes in the lives of people. Leading corporations have created new markets for their services and products by including the poorer people in both rural and urban areas in their schemes for growth of their businesses. Thereby, they have also brought knowledge, incomes, and hope to many poorer sections of society.

The change in the role of the government in development has also been critical. Several government officers have been good enablers of change. They have supported the communities by removing obstacles and facilitating access to the requisite resources by the communities.

In many parts of the country, the attitude of people towards responsibility for producing the desired changes is very heartening. People are working together—communities, businesses, government, and non-government agencies—to produce the change that everybody desires. While in some parts of the country the pace of change has yet to accelerate, we are no longer despondent. We know how it can be done. It is being done, and we have results that speak for this reality.

Where are the leaders?

Whenever I present this broad-brush vision of India's future, someone is likely to say that it is an inspiring vision but there is a problem. 'What about leadership? Where are the leaders?' I respond with two questions of my own: What is 'leadership'? And who is a 'leader'?

I have a simple definition of leadership: A leader is she or he who takes the first steps towards something that she or he deeply cares about, and in ways that others wish to follow. That could not be all, some people think. What about charisma? And, what is my list of the seven or eight essential characteristics of leaders? I ask these people to reflect on the essence of leadership. They agree that, by definition, leaders move ahead of others or they would be followers. On reflection, they agree that leaders find their direction from their own deeper aspiration, and not from surveys of the crowd's opinions.

I often ask people to pause, be silent for a moment, and consider what they care about most deeply. It is surprising how often people will say that they never ever really do this. Therefore they cannot know if they are merely shuffling along, following the crowd. The first, and essential, step to becoming a leader then has to be the discovery of one's own deep 'Know-Wants'.

The other half of the definition is equally important. If there are no followers, there is no leader. Leaders can exercise power over people in many ways. The power can spring from their position in the hierarchy, or from their wealth, or from their power to coerce with the use of force. CEOs and army generals have the power of position. Owners of enterprises have the power of wealth. Dictators have the power that, in Mao's words, springs from the barrel of a gun. But the best leaders do not have any of these sources of power, and yet people follow them nevertheless.

My favourite image of leadership is the statue of Mahatma Gandhi on Sardar Patel Marg in New Delhi. A man dressed in a simple dhoti and slippers, a staff in hand, stepping out purposefully. Behind him many people follow. He is not their boss. He has no wealth to share with them. His staff is not there to threaten them. Yet they follow him. Because they too care for the cause.

India has many leaders, in its villages, on its factory floors, in its schools, and in many other walks of life. These are people who are taking steps towards what they care about and in ways that others around them wish to follow. And India has many millions more with the potential to lead. These are the 'tiny ripples of hope' and 'million different centres of energy' that Robert Kennedy spoke about that can create a mighty current. These are the millions of 'fireflies' that will make India really shine.

Bibliography

Arndt, HW: *Economic Development: The History of an Idea*, University of Chicago Press, Chicago, 1989.

Blanchard, Kenneth & Johnson Spencer: *The One Minute Manager*, New York: William Morrow and Company, Inc., 1982.

de Soto, Hernando: *The Mystery of Capital—Why Capitalism Triumphs in the West and Fails Everywhere Else.* London: Bantam Press, Transworld Publishers, W5 55A, 244 pages, 2000.

Emmott, Bill: *20:21 Vision: Twentieth-Century Lessons for the Twenty-first Century.* New York: Farrar, Straus & Giroux, 2003.

Fauconnier, H & Eric Sutton: *The Soul of Malaya*, Kuala Lumpur, Oxford University Press, 1965.

Hammer, Michael & James Champy: *Reengineering the Corporation*, New York, HarperBusiness. 1993.

Hochschild, Arlie: 'The Nanny Chain,' *The American Prospect*, Vol. 11, No. 4, January 3, 2000.

Lakoff, George: *Moral Politics: What Conservatives Know That Liberals Don't*, University of Chicago Press, 1996.

Lala, RM: *The Creation of Wealth: The Tata Story*, New Delhi: IBH Publishers, 1992.

Maira, Arun: *Shaping the Future: Aspirational Leadership in India and Beyond.* New York, Wiley, 2002.

Manfredi, Valerio Massimo: *Alexander: Ends of the Earth Vol. 3*, Washington: Washington Square Press, 2002.

Micklethwait, John & Adrian Wooldridge: *The Company—A Short History of a Revolutionary Idea*, Modern Library Chronicles, Modern Library; Modern edition, 2003.

Naipaul, VS: *An Area of Darkness: A Discovery of India*, Knopf Publishing Group, London, 2002.

Neustadt, Richard & Ernest May. *Thinking In Time: The Uses of History for Decision-Makers*. New York, The Free Press, 1986.

Peter, B, Scott, Morgan & Arun Maira: *The Accelerating Organization: Embracing the Human Face of Change*, McGraw-Hill Education, New York, 1997.

Sandel, Michael J: *Democracy's Discontent: America in Search of a Public Philosophy*, Harvard University Press, 1996.

Senge, Peter M: *The Fifth Discipline: The Art & Practice of The Learning Organization*, New York, Currency Doubleday, 1990.

Senge, Peter M, Art Kleiner, Charlotte Roberts, Rick Ross, George Roth & Bryan Smith: *The Dance of Change: The Challenges of Sustaining Momentum in Learning Organizations*, New York, Doubleday, 1999.

Thurow, Lester: *Fortune Favours the Bold*, London, HarperBusiness, 2003.

Turner, Adair: *Just Capital—The Liberal Economy*, Macmillan, 2001.

Warren G Bennis & Robert J Thomas: *Geeks and Geezers: How Era, Values, and Defining Moments Shape Leaders*, HBSP, Harvard, 2002.

Zakaria, Fareed: *The Future of Freedom: Illiberal Democracy at Home and Abroad*, WW Norton & Company, April 2003.

Index

Accelerating Organisation: Embracing the Human Face of Change, by Arun Maira and Peter Scott-Morgan, 55
acceleration, 84
accomplishment, 104
after-sale service, 170–1
Ahluwalia, Montek Singh, 57
Air India, 88
Alexander, 96, 112, 119, 120
alienation, 139
alignment, 27, 72, 85, 216, 218, 221, 224
appreciating returns, principle of, 60
Argyris, Chris, 82, 126
Aristotle, 202
Arthur D Little Inc (ADL), 47, 54, 109–10
Arthur, Brian, 60
Aspen Institute, 132, 134–35, 136
aspirations, 82, 96, 104, 108; and concepts, 167–72
attitude, change, 110, 171
authoritarian power, 215
authority, 85

Bangalore Action Task Force (BATF), 176, 177
bargaining, 165
behaviours, 82, 110
beliefs and concepts, 82, 85, 172
Bendahara, Tengku Arif, 97–102, 103
'Benedict Arnold', 153
Bennis, Warren, 96
Bharat Petroleum Corporation Ltd (BPCL), 55
Bharatiya Janata Party (BJP), 15–16, 125
Blanchard, *One Minute Manager*, 197
Bombay Plan, 37
Boston Consulting Group (BCG), 17
brand building process, 101
British Petroleum, 139
British: exploitation of India, 36
bureaucrats, bureaucracy, 44, 45, 57, 58, 186–87
Bush, George (Sr), 185
business and the nation building, 17–21

business community, 38–9
business leaders, role, 135
business methods, efficacy, 174
business sector, role in society, 31–2
businessmen, 186, 187

capability-related promotions, 165
capitalism, 29–30, 65, 87, 88, 131–32, 139
caste, 192
Cementos Mexicana (Cemex), 50–3
change process, 19–20, 50, 80, 84–85, 109, 177–79; human face, 54–58; resistance to, 82, 166
change-ability, 164
China, 26; polity, 84
Choksi, Prof, 40, 50
civil society, 32, 152, 186, 220
coalition government, 15–18, 23
collective action, 113
collective behaviour, 80
colonialism, 114
commercial vehicle industry, 105
commitment, 85, 104, 115–17, 178, 223–5
communication, 112, 114, 139, 144–45, 184–85, 189–95; *See also* information and communication technology, internet and communication technology
communism, 30, 132
community participation, 27
companies and society, relations, 30–1

competence, 143
competition, 50, 52, 99, 104, 106, 115, 147, 186
competitive advantage, 26, 53, 155; market, 64; spirit, 203
competitiveness, 148, 151
concepts, 159–60; and actions, 160–67
conceptual challenge, 143, 145
conceptual emergencies, 138–46, 149
Confederation of Indian Industry (CII), 116, 186–87
confidence, 43–44
conflict and experimentation process, 149
Congress, 15–16
connectivity infrastructure, 213
consciousness, 39
consensus, 19
conservatism, 130
cooperation, 27, 48, 110, 174
coordination, 70
corporate(s): imperialism, 69; social responsibility, 30
corporations, 17–18
corruption, 25, 90
creative tension, concept of, 105, 108
creativity process, 82, 164
culture, 115, 146; change, 50–53
customer(s), customer's: care, 171; confidence, 101; credibility, 213; focus, 55; perspective, 169; relations, 48
cynicism, 38

Daimler Benz, 93, 95, 98, 164

Dalai Lama, 196
Das, Tarun, 57
debating, 203
decision-making, 142; process, 18
degradation, 30
Deming, Dr, 161
democracy, 15, 23, 24, 27, 64, 141–43, 151, 201
demographic trends, 155
Deng Xiao Ping, 179
development, 16–20, 36– 38, 57, 72, 88, 114–16, 118, 129, 131–32, 135, 148–51, 201, 204, 213, 221, 223, 226
developmental institutions, 114
devotion, 184
dialogue, process of, 28, 84–85, 152, 175, 203–4
diminishing costs, law of, 60
disorder, 165
diversity, 26–27, 144, 145, 148, 151, 172, 193, 200–1
downloading, 203
downsizing, 68, 174
downward spiral, 215
Drucker, Peter, 190
Dutt Industrial Policy Enquiry Committee, 39
dynamism, 155

ecological sustainability, 148
economic development, growth, 17, 83, 85, 114, 132, 144, 150, 152, 204, 210–2, 219
economic reforms process, 16–17, 19, 56, 64, 187
economy, economic factors, 15–16, 20, 22–23, 38, 44, 64, 68, 113, 125–26, 137, 154–5

education, education system, 15, 27, 90, 186, 188, 225–26; inadequacy, 221–22; and training, 213; value-based, 90
efficacy, 213
electoral calculus, 16
emotional, emotions, 105, 202; motivation, 218; needs, 218
employment, 154–55
empowerment, 28, 179
endemic problems, 221–22
Enlightenment, 199
Enron, 119, 120
entrepreneurship, 86, 156
entropy, 166
environmental degradation, 23, 139–40; management, 218
evolution process, 150, 165
excellence, 74, 76, 88, 115
exploration, 205

family values, 130–1
fashion, 64–65
federalism, 148
Federation of Indian Chambers of Commerce and Industry (FICCI), 39, 40
financial performance, 49
Fireflies Arising, 210, 225–28
Ford Motor Company, 190
Foreign Direct Investment (FDI), 64, 147, 155
foreign exchange crisis, 186
fragmentation, 139, 192
freedom, 132
free-market paradigm, free trade, 148–49, 153
Friedman, Milton, 88

Fritz, Robert, 82, 105
frustration, 80, 204, 214–15, 221
Fukuyama, Francis, 29, 58

Gandhi, Indira, 44, 183, 184
Gandhi, MK, 36, 44, 143, 183
Gandhi, Rajiv, 17, 44
Garvin, David, 54
Geneen, Harold, 119, 120
General Electric (GE), 120
General Motors (GM), 100, 162–63
Global Business Network, 56
global: capitalism, 132; economy, 83; governance, 205
globalisation, 120, 129, 131–33, 135, 136, 144, 153
goals, 96, 117
government, governance, 83, 145, 186–88; role in development, 37–38, 135
Grameen Bank, 71
gross domestic product (GDP), 116, 129, 144, 147, 154
growth, 147, 148, 154, 156
Growth Competitiveness Index, 220

Harley-Davidson, 167–68
Harvard Business School, 54
helplessness, 26, 27, 215
heterogeneity, 130
High Level Strategic Group (HLSG), 212–3, 223
high leverage initiative to accelerate change, 210, 213–8
Hindustan Machine Tools (HMT), 42

Hino, 100, 104
Hitler, Adolf, 141
Hochschild, Arlie, 136
Honda, 167
Human Development Index, 220
human resource management, 97
human resource systems, 165–66
hypocrisy, 89

idealism, 36
improvement process, 173, 174, 176–77, 223–24
incentives, 165–66
inclusiveness, 16
Indian Administrative Service (IAS), 37, 38, 39
Indian Civil Service (ICS), 37
Indian Foreign Service (IFS), 37, 38, 39
Indian Institutes of Management (IIMs), 61
Indian Institutes of Technology (IITs), 38, 61
industrial development strategy, 42
industrial licensing regulations, 187
industrial revolution, 210
information, information and communication technologies, 59, 60, 70, 172, 177–78, 189–92, 197; economy, 60; right to, 178; *See also* internet and communication technology
Infosys, 176
infrastructure, 73–74, 173
initiative to make a difference, 210, 218–23

Innovation Associates, USA, 54, 82
innovations, innovative strategies, 25, 53, 70–72, 82, 108, 118, 156, 163, 168
insights, 56, 57
integration, 139
interdisciplinary problems, 218
international competition, 51
International Council of Executive Development Research (ICEDR), USA, 164
International Futures Forum, St Andrews, Scotland, 139, 149, 193
International Monetary Fund (IMF), 150, 201
internet and communication technology, 58, 59, 70, 112, 155, 225
interstate commerce, 156
inventory management, 161–64
investments, 147
involvement, 179
Irani, Jamshed, 111
Ishikawa, Dr, 161, 167, 194

Jalan, Bimal, 87–88, 192
Jamshedpur, 133–34
Japan, Japanese, 104–6; automobiles, 47; competition with Indian industry, 45, 58, 166–68; organizations, 160–1; quality management, 163, 167, 194
Japanese Union of Scientists and Engineers (JUSE), 194
Johnson, Lyndon B., 190

'Just Do It', 65, 117–18
Just-in-Time (JIT), 80

Kahane, Adam, 56
Kalam, APJ Abdul, 25, 116
kanban, 162
Kantor, David, 131
Kennedy, John F, 190
Kennedy, Robert, 228
Ken Saro-Wiwa, Nigeria, 32
Kiefer, Charlie, 54
Know-Hows, 172
Know-Wants, 85, 112, 172
Know-Whats, 172
Know-Whys, 85, 112, 172
knowledge, 54, 79, 173, 222
knowledge management, 82
Kumble, Anil, 159–60

labour laws, 19, 56, 156
labour reforms, 23
Lakoff, George, 130–1
Lay, Kenneth, 119
leadership, leaders, 19, 24, 96, 151, 179, 225–8; models, 174
Learning Field, 79–82
learning organization, 165
learning process, 53, 80, 96, 160, 167, 171, 172
Levin, Jerry, 198
liberalisation of economy, 56–57, 63, 87, 186
liberalism, 130
licensing, 58, 97
limited liability company, concept of, 30
listening, 192–95; barriers to, 190
literacy, 63

Malaysia: government policy, 97–98; *See also* Tatab Industries, Malaysia
management, 19, 48, 49, 71, 72, 149, 189
managers and shareholders, relations, 30
'managing India brainstorm', 175
Manfredi, Valerio, 120
manpower development, 95
manufacturing management, 160–62, 164
manufacturing sector, 80, 156
market, market forces', 121, 139, 155–56, 167, 187
Mashelkar, Dr, 25
Massachusetts Institute of Technology (MIT), 129, 203
Mavericks, Dallas, 86–88
Mazda, 106
McLuhan, 185
McNamara, Robert, 190
media, role, 135, 191
mental models, 131
Mercedes, 168–71
Mercedes Benz, 42, 104, 169
middle-class, 62
mindfulness, 139
mindset change, 18, 167
misconceptions, 189
Mitsubishi, 106
mixed economy, 37
moderation, 191
modernities, 145
money, 87
Monopolies Inquiry Commission, 39

Minsky, Harold, 65, 132 (sp variation)
Moolgaokar, Sumant, 42, 46, 48, 54, 74, 93–101, 161
Moore, Thomas, 60
moral issues, 136
Morris, Errol, 190
motivation, 50, 114, 120–1, 145
multinational corporations (MNCs), 164
Muthuraman, B, 111, 112

Naipaul, VS, 43, 75–76, 97
national conversation, 222–3
negotiation process, 205
Nehru, Jawahar Lal, 36, 37, 44
Nesbitt, Richard, 130
networked enterprises, 70–71
new economy, 58–60, 69
Nilekani, Nandan, 176–77
Nissan, 106
non-governmental organisations (NGOs), 31, 115, 177, 201, 221, 225
Non-Resident Indian (NRI), 117
North American Free Trade Agreement (NAFTA), 50
North Atlantic Treaty Organization (NATO), 138–39, 143
Nye, Joseph, 204

O'Neil, Tip, 153
objectivity, 137
official process, 204–05
offshore concept acceptability, 213
Olson, 72
open society, 23
opinion polls, 185

organisational issues, 69–70
organisational learning, 18, 19, 54–55, 72, 79–80
organisational performance, 79
organising and governing, new model, 70–72
orthodoxy, 149
'over the wall', 107

Palkhiwala, Nani, 99, 100–1
parliamentary process, 220–1
participation process, 16, 19–20, 24, 57, 117, 187, 205
passion, 159–60
people and corporations, relations, 69
perfection, 74
performance, 52, 53, 76, 80, 114, 160, 162–63, 216
performance improvement, 49, 54–55, 115, 163–64
persistence, 94
Peters, Tom, 196–7
philanthropy, 32
physical infrastructure, poor quality, 221
planning, planning process, 19, 213, 218; for commitment, not compliance, 210, 223–25; and management, 217–18
Planning Commission, 57
policy changes, 156
policy-making, 192, 217
political process, system, politics, politicians, 16, 18, 44, 56, 68, 90, 153, 178, 186–87, 191
political will, 187
population growth, 64

Porus, defeated by Alexander, 96
poverty, 23, 24, 25, 27, 30–2, 62, 63, 84, 139, 151, 211, 220
power, 121
Prahalad, CK, 116
predictability, 164
prediction and control, 217
prices, 56, 64
private capitalism and state socialism, struggle, 29
private sector, 31, 37–8, 68
privatisation, 187
problem solving, 163
process engineering, 52
process improvement, 52
product development, 107, 166
production process, 166, 167
productivity, 48, 49, 51, 211; improvement, 173
Project Jupiter, 107–8, 165
public policy and governance, 31
public sector enterprises (PSUs), 64, 126
public sector, 37–38, 187
public-private partnership, 213
public systems, 90
purchasing power parity (PPP), 129

quality, 48, 49, 84, 106, 163, 167, 194, 224; improvement, 164; and quality, 136–38

Rangan, Kasturi, 175
rationality, 214, 216
Ravi Shankar, 159–60
Reddy, Anji, 175
reengineering, 164, 172

reflection, 110
reform process, 221
religions, 117, 192
religious divisiveness, 16
resources, resource allocation, 19,
    210–13
respect, 110
rethinking, 53
rights, 201, 203
Robertson, George, 138–39, 143
role models, 90
Royal Dutch Shell, 56
Rumsfeld, Donald, 23
rural agricultural economy, 156

Sachs, Goldman, 154
Salim Ali, 94
Sandel, Michael, 132, 136
scenario planning, 56, 72
Scharmer, Otto, 203
Scottish Council Foundation, 139
Scott-Morgan, Peter, 54
secularism, 116
self-deception, 190
self-interest, selfishness, 88, 89, 90,
    148, 216, 220
Sen, Amartya, 132
Senge, Peter, 54, 82, 105; *The
    Fifth Discipline*, 197
service experience, 213
*Shaping the Future: Aspirational
    Leadership in India and Beyond*,
    by Arun Maira, 58
shared aspirations,159
shared visions, 84–85, 105, 117,
    121, 172; and vision shared,
    distinction, 109–12
Sharma, MD, 94–95

Shell, 32
shoddiness, 73
Shourie, Arun, 25
Silicon Valley, 59, 61, 69, 116
Singapore: Economic Develop-
    ment Board, 150; transforma-
    tion, 176
Singh, Manmohan, 16–17, 44, 57,
    186–87
skilled workforce, 211–12
skills, 23, 55, 96, 159, 172
Smith, Adam, 139
social development, 32
social equity, 148
social issues, 31, 32, 68
socialism, 65, 135
societal learning, 79, 80, 82, 151
Society of Indian Automobile
    Manufacturers (SIAM), 26
socio-economic implications, 212
socio-political-economic system,
    174, 213–18
socio-technical system, 52–53
Socrates, 202
software development, 134
South Africa, Mont Fleur Project,
    56; transition process, 28
Soviet Union, collapse, 29, 120;
    private sector, 38; model of
    planning, 37
spirit, 97, 168
stability, 164
stakeholders, diversity, 23
state, 29
stock market, 60, 59, 126
strategies, 154
stress, 102

structural differences, 174
subsidies, 19, 56, 64, 174
Sunderajan, U, 55, 111
surplus, 32
Swiss Institute of Management Development, 147
systems change, 171
systems thinking, 217

tabloidisation, 191
Tagore, Rabindranath, 193
Tata Administrative Services (TAS), 40, 50
Tata Consultancy Services (TCS), 134
Tata Group, Tatas, 17, 40–45, 55, 88, 90, 93, 98–104, 133–34, 150, 171
Tata, JRD, 40, 46, 54, 55, 87–88, 90, 96, 133
Tata Motors (Telco), 36, 41, 42, 43, 45, 46, 58, 74–75, 93–95, 97–99, 102, 105–6, 108, 164, 166–67, 184
Tata, Ratan N, 46
Tata Steel, 88, 111, 133–34
Tatab Industries, Malaysia, 97–102, 108, 168–71
teamwork, 79, 80, 102, 104–5, 108, 163
technical process, 166
technical skills, 76
Teerlink, Richard, 167–68
TELCO, *See* Tata Motors telecommunications, 156; infrastructure, 225
terrorism, 23, 24, 139, 143
theory-in-use, 84, 121, 126, 143
thermodynamics, 165–66

Thomas, Robert, 96
Thurow, Lester, 129–30, 131
Time Warner, 198
Time-Life, 198
top-down change process, 177
total quality management (TQM), 75, 80, 194
Toyota, 100, 104, 106, 167, 169; production system, 161–63; Corolla (Car Model Name), 169
trade barriers, 50
trade unions, 192
training, 79, 80, 164
transformation, 27, 83, 115, 149, 176
trust, trustworthiness, 32, 103, 140, 142–3
Tully, Mark, 116
Turner, Adair, 150

understanding, 143, 189–92
unemployment, 64, 113, 211
United Nations, 141
United States of America: capitalism, 58–59; corporate scandals, 29, 30; democracy, 24; economy, 153; employment, 153; industry, 47; property rights, 150–1; terrorist attack on 9/11, 23
unity, 148; values, 88
utilities, prices, 19

Vajpayee, Atal Behari, 65
value system, values, 86–90, 152
violence, 139, 143–4, 145, 204–5

F/ANE 18/06.

vision, 19–20, 27, 28, 90, 111, 112, 116, 117, 121, 133, 165, 167–68, 175, 194
Vivian Bose Commission, 39

Wanchoo Committee, 39
Warner Brothers, 198
Watson, 72
Ways of Mass Dialogue (WMD), 200, 204
weapons of mass destruction, (WMD), 200, 201
wisdom, 138, 144, 197
work processes, 53, 172
working age population, 154
working prototype, 167

World Affairs, 145
World Bank, 150
World Economic Forum (WEF), 147
World Trade Organisation (WTO), 201
World War II, 150, 194
World Wrestling Federation (WWF), 196–98

xenophobia, 16

Yamaha, 167

Zakaria, Fareed, 141–42
Zambrano, Lorenzo, 51–53